THE RUGBY COACHING MANUAL

RUGBY UNLOCKED AND IT'S NOT ROCKET SCIENCE

by Keith Richardson
Editor Stephen Jones

The Rugby Coaching Manual

Rugby Unlocked - And It's Not Rocket Science

by Keith Richardson
Editor Stephen Jones

First published in 2010   ISBN: 978-0-9566171-0-1

1st Edition ©Copyright 2010 by Keith Richardson

This Edition published by Keith Richardson www.thercm.org

CONTENTS

Introduction

ABOUT THE AUTHOR

The author started his rugby-playing career under Don Broughton, the PE teacher at George Stephenson Grammar School, Westmoor, Newcastle on Tyne and played club rugby as a schoolboy for Seghill.

He went to Loughborough (1961–64) and was coached by J. D. Robins, then played for Rosslyn Park and Bath before joining Gloucester in 1969. He started there as a No 8 but soon became converted to prop and stayed in that position till his retirement from playing. He captained Gloucester and coached them for many years before moving as Head Coach to Harlequins, Newbury then Coventry.

He coached South West Division, England Emerging Players, England 'A' and England U21 and is a Level IV RFU coach who was Editor of the RFU Technical Journal 2001 – 2008.

ABOUT THE EDITOR

Stephen Jones has been rugby correspondent of the Sunday Times for 25 years and in that time has become known as one of the leading rugby commentators in the world. He has been sports correspondent of the year in the Sport England awards on three occasions, won the Sports Story of the Year in 2006 and in 2005, was chosen as the UK Sports Journalist of the Year.

INTRODUCTION

Being a 'rugby coach' will mean many things to many people and each coach will have a different agenda. Some will be working at a level where players' improvement and development is of paramount importance, but there are many who will be judged on each Saturday's result.

No coaching advice or instruction can satisfy all requirements all of the time, but there has to be a practical way of assisting coaches with vastly different needs - and the many in between who want results *and* player development to go hand-in-hand.

There is a tendency in the game to over-elaborate and try to make the whole coaching process far more complex and theoretical than it really is. There are certain key elements in rugby and they have to be mastered, but over-elaboration from the coach to his Saturday players will probably end in disappointment and failure.

I have been to many coaching courses and presentations over many years and the simple truth always emerges that simple things done well tend to work best; ideas that require a university degree to work them out generally fail. However, that does not suggest that simple ideas cannot be improved upon; the successful coach will be trying to get the 'edge' with such a philosophy of doing the simple things well. Work out the basics then refine, practise and develop them so that your team is better at them than anybody else.

Coaching is probably what you will do least, in actual time spent, in your coaching duties. It is alarming how many seemingly irrelevant matters take up time, yet it is a problem that is generally only realised after the event(s). Coaching courses, rightly, usually deal with pure coaching practice and theory; this book is an attempt to add some practical advice to the excellent material already available through the national body's coaching schemes.

Many coaches become almost obsessed with drills and practices without looking at the fundamentals of the game. You can run players through drills till they are exhausted, but they will probably not understand the game any better at the end of the session.

This book is an attempt to demystify the essentials of the game and present them in relatively simple language. A good coach needs to understand what the game is all about before he can have any meaningful impact on his players' development. He must first understand the game himself then pass on awareness of what it all means to his team. Hopefully, this book will clear up certain misunderstandings in this complex game.

CHAPTER 1

CONSIDER YOUR COACHING STYLE AND MEET THE PLAYERS

You will be spending many hours in your coaching duties and you will be rewarded by carefully considering *how* you will coach. A useful starting point might be to read Lynn Kidman's excellent book 'Athlete-centred Coaching' (details at end of chapter 1). This may well guide you towards a style of coaching that can be more rewarding and profitable than a simpler 'do this because I said so' approach.

When you are considering this matter of coaching style, meet the players and ask them what they want to aim for in the coming season; by calling this meeting, you have already started on a regime of athlete-centred coaching. At this pre-season stage their aspirations will probably prove to be over-optimistic, but there is absolutely nothing wrong with optimism and it is more useful to any team than a dose of cynicism. You will only be able to tell if their ambitions were over-optimistic after the team has played a few matches.

Try to introduce realism without dampening their enthusiasm as you ask the players to suggest achievable codes of conduct on such matters as training, time-keeping, communication, kit at training and matches, training habits, personal and team discipline and how they, the players, would ideally like to deal with these issues. At this pre-season discussion stage, they will probably promise to be very harsh on the slightest misdemeanour, so do try to go for aims that are achievable – then you and they must work very hard to stick to those rules and guidelines.

This initial meeting can set the tone for your coming season and may offer an opportunity for you to think even further about how you will coach. You have brought the players into this first discussion; why not try to maintain their involvement throughout the playing season as well? You could shout a lot and run a strict coaching regime that is mainly drill-based. If, however, your aim is to improve your players in the long-term, a player empowerment and involvement process may well provide bigger gains. That does not mean that you let players decide how the coaching will be organised, but you might be surprised at what your players can offer if you pose problems rather than providing answers all the time. Show that you value players' contributions; you will not be showing weakness.

One important item to discuss may be training nights, especially if they have traditionally been on Monday and Thursday. If this is the club routine, suggest that Tuesday is generally better than twenty four hours earlier as players' bodies have an extra day to recover and training can be harder with (probably) more fit players present.

Pyramid. After you have had a first meeting and you have some idea of what the players see as achievable aims, it is well worth going through a very simple process with them and ask them to fill in the bits and pieces that maintain and support the sporting equivalent of a pyramid. Have a pyramid shape on a sheet of paper or whiteboard with something like 'success and performance' at the top of the shape. (A flip-chart is useful as it can be easily carried to any venue in future if you need to use it as a training or pre-match motivational aid).

DIAGRAM 1

PERFORMANCE
SUCCESS

UNDERSTAND GAME.
POSSESSION. GOAL KICKING.
PACE. WILLING TO ATTACK.
AGGRESSIVE DEFENCE SKILL.
HARD YARDS. GO-FORWARD.
FITNESS. TEAM SPIRIT. DETERMINATION

Invite the players to consider what will be needed to allow and support that 'success and performance'. You may have to direct the thought processes but generally the players will come up with the appropriate answers. Graft, effort, organisation, commitment, team play, working for each other, clear vision of where the team is going and training as you would play in a game are what you may be offered, though there are many more valid answers. Rugby relies on all of these qualities; without the sweat in training and games, skill will simply remain wrapped up and largely unused because your team will not have a great deal of possession to play with.

A major factor in any team's success could be the choice of captain. The club may have a system so check out what it is. Your own choice is best but you may not yet know the players well enough. Is there any real need to have a captain yet? Is the speed of naming one mainly due to the fact that the committee wants to print the captain's name on the fixture list? This is possibly the main reason for any haste, so stick out for what *you* want. If you want to see the players in action before a captain is announced, go for that and be bulldog-jawed about it. It is, after all, a minor issue at this stage, but there may be a dedicated group of committeemen whose sole function is to name the captain; beware of such dignitaries and meet them head-on as early as you can. You will often get your way if you show strength from the outset; lose early skirmishes and the later battles become really tough.

If you really don't know whom you want and/or it doesn't bother you, let the players vote – then they have picked their man and are collectively responsible for that decision. There will have to be rules on who can vote or the process becomes dangerous; you do not want a no-hoper becoming captain because his mates thought it might be a nice touch after his forty years' service at prop. Whatever you do, though, fight to the bitter end to stop the club and/or the committee having a say if you can. They don't have to play with him and they may well go on that well known method of selection - Buggins' Turn. The captain is your voice on and off the pitch so get this one right at the start, whether it was you or the players who made the choice.

Leadership comes in many forms and it is not necessarily the loudest voice who is the best. What is important, however, is that the rest of the players know that their captain is a "Come on" and not a "Go on" type of player. He may play in a position, say the wing, where there are not as many opportunities to get physically involved as there might be at flanker, but the team has to know that he is up for it when his time comes; it is crucial that they respect his 'bottle' as well as his team talks and skill levels.

You soon get to know what your players are made of, though pre-season gives only a partial profile. The heat of real rugby games is where you really find out what individuals are made of. You can use a battlefield image to assess certain players, certainly your captain, and, though unscientific, it might give you a quick pen-portrait of somebody if you have not yet chosen your captain. Ask yourself the simple question: "Would I want to be in the same trench as this man?" If your answer is a resounding no, why should the rest of the players want him by their side when the match gets tough, especially if he was originally chosen to lead by example?

Some clubs have a curious position known as the Vice Captain. This is usually the first player you drop, so beware. The post is probably not needed at all and is only there because the club has had one since whenever they were formed. A better system is to appoint people to areas of responsibility to help the captain on the pitch. You will see such leadership assistants emerge as the training and the season go along. Make the process unofficial but pay attention to these lieutenants – they may have a wealth of experience and nous. An old hand to look after the scrum, lineout, restarts and defence can be a useful foursome – but develop the system with care – there is no rush and you need to get it right.

At this stage it may be worth setting out a strategy that the team and club will employ during the coming season and that relates to how the referee is treated. You will not get the referee on your side so that you always win by being falsely pleasant to the official. But you might enjoy a better game if the referee is treated like a fellow human being by the whole club, especially the players on the pitch. Try to formulate a sensible and socially acceptable system with your players before the first game. All players feel that they are being harshly treated by the man with the whistle at some stage of most games, but he is the sole judge of Law for the span of each and every encounter and he is not likely to change a decision because players suggest that he was wrong.

You might consider asking a referee to come to your practice sessions. You might have one within the club, certainly somebody who lives not far away. Get him and let him referee certain aspects of what you are doing. The players should become used to being whistled for errors and they might just accept Saturday's decisions with better grace than if they were to regard the referee as an alien species.

Bring the committee in on this as they can have a big part to play. Ensure that somebody meets the referee and shows him, at least, where the changing rooms are. After the game, have somebody who is responsible for getting him to the clubhouse, even though it is obvious to you where it is. And ensure that at least your captain and you have a chat about the match over a drink. You may have to force yourself to go through with it, but it is a discipline that the game at large needs. And you might start to realise that his interpretation might have been right – or more right than yours!

(Lynn Kidman's books: Athlete-Centred Coaching, ISBN 0-476-01445-X; Athlete-Centred Coaching 2nd edition, ISBN 0-9565065-0-4; Developing Decision Makers, ISBN 0-473-07587-3)

CHAPTER 2

COACHING FUNDAMENTALS

The first idea to throw out of the coaching window is that coaches of the top players do something that is beyond you and your players; they don't. What they do is to develop the basic skills to a degree that you haven't got time for and your players probably haven't the desire or the naturally high starting point of talent from which to aspire. The skills that underpin rugby are very straightforward but must never take a back seat in any coach's programme. If you want to practise complex 'state of the art' moves, you will not get very far if your players cannot catch and pass; and if the receiver has no idea of lines of running to come onto the pass to beat an opponent, the move is wasted from the outset. It is almost built-in obsolescence, as it will nearly always fail.

You may well develop a 'slant' on *how* a certain skill can be coached and that is encouraging as innovative coaches are thin on the ground. However, the nuts and bolts of the skill will almost certainly be precisely the same as the skill being coached in thousands of clubs worldwide. If you can develop your method, however, go for it; it has as much chance of success as anybody else's and yours may well be the best way to go about the issue.

Whatever you come up with, there is one basic truth in the game and the way it is played; your team has to get the ball in front of most of your players at some stage or you are doomed. There are not too many ways to achieve this and the obvious ones are running/handling, kicking and tackling an opponent behind the majority of his own players. Much hot air has been spouted on how complex the game is, but this truth is self-evident at all levels of the game and the sooner you can achieve the go-forward momentum the better. A team that spends too many chunks of the game running backwards before they can start to run forwards is a team that, in all probability, is going to lose. So you need to get this simple template firmly etched in yours and the players' minds before you start to tinker with the fine detail of the shape of your game.

The initial sources of possession from set-piece scrum and lineout are as good a starting point as any to start getting the ball in front of the team and the breakdown principles can follow in a natural progression. If you lose sight of the hugely important initial set-piece ball, you have not taken on board that it is one of the few times in the game when about half of the opposition is virtually in the same spot and immobile. So your first thoughts should be on how you will win your own set-piece ball and how to get it in front of that point as quickly as possible. Much will depend on personnel available, so watch your players closely in pre-season and weigh up who might be able to offer what in this vital department.

Your restart should really be considered a set-piece that you will regain and not give up lamely to the opposition; unfortunately, it is rarely accurate enough to be seen as near-certain possession. Practise it as often as you can and, when there is a degree of competence and regularity, add it to your team's set-piece 'should win' ball.

CHAPTER 3

PRE-SEASON TRAINING

It is a good idea to plan the shape of your sessions before you ever start. Players will generally want to have a pretty casual game of touch at the start to get themselves warm and ready for when the latecomers arrive. Avoid their version of **touch-rugby** and introduce your own version of what you want at the first meeting; introduce a sensible game and do not allow a loose mess of what we usually see.

Your game needs to serve a purpose by demanding skills and concentration. One option is for the ball carrier to stop when he is touched. This can be refereed by one player or you can have the game stopped as soon as the defending player shouts, "Touch!" There will be arguments, but they have to play with unfair decisions each Saturday so it is not a bad training method. The player with the ball has to stop quickly after the touch, stand with feet astride and play the ball immediately backwards between his legs, using both hands to push the ball backwards and slightly upwards. If he uses only one hand, raises one foot, passes above his body height as he is bending down or the ball hits the floor, possession is turned over. You soon develop straight running lines and there is always the option to add rules as the game progresses – e.g. minimum of 2 passes before a break, miss pass(es), so many decoy runners etc. This will be far more demanding than the game that the players want to play.

The **basic handling, passing and running skills** that you will coach and nurture are important and the players need to know what you are talking about from the start. There are basics that all players need and lines of running principles are vital. You may have problems with this as many players agree with you conversationally but lose the plot as soon as they get a ball in their hand. The theory of aiming for the immediate defender's inside shoulder is so simple as to be laughable, but why do your players understand that, yet run towards the touchline when they get the ball?

In your skill practices, do try to avoid the players starting in a straight line; this is so far removed from what usually happens in the chaos and turmoil in a game and rarely, if ever, will they start in this position during the eighty minutes on Saturday. By all means let the players learn what is required in the practice, but disorientate them slightly as soon as possible by first running them into a tackle, round a cone or through some poles. This has the effect of making players work and look to get to the best spot for the practice and it adds a valuable dimension to their game. At the same time encourage your players *not* to carry on with the move, practice or drill if it feels wrong or they know that the other players are out of position. This is part and parcel of getting game-related responses in training, which might just translate into good practice in club games. Stress the important point that it is rarely beneficial to anybody but the opposition to carry on passing 'cock-up' ball; make sure that your players understand this simple, but often overlooked, aspect of the game. If the ball-carrier senses that all is not well, suggest that he simply runs through to touch down at the end of the working grid or that he simply passes to a well-placed but 'wrong' player who happens to be available.

There are enough drills and practices around, but one little practice impressed me as holding all the core essentials in handling, passing and beating defenders whilst **preserving the outside space**. This outside space is all too easily eaten into or totally lost by players running laterally and its preservation is a vital aspect of effective game management. It is, however, a skill that requires constant vigil from the coach at all aspects of training as it is so simple for players to drift across without being fully aware of what they are doing and how they are adversely affecting their attacking options. Video can be very useful, especially if the camera films from the goal posts and not the touchline, so that the line of run from the first receiver can be seen to be crucial in virtually everything else that happens afterwards – on the training pitch from the first pre-season session to in-season practice sessions.

DIAGRAM 2

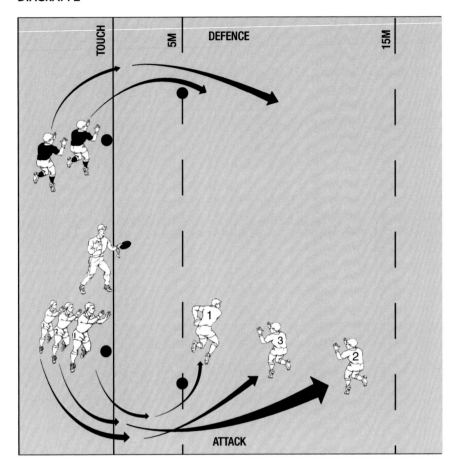

The coach is at the heart of all the work and he decides on the pace of things.

There are three attackers each time and they run backwards around a cone before the first runner takes the coach's pass to attack.

As the attackers start, two defenders run backwards around their entry cone before they come in to defend.

You can have one single line of players and they take turns to go off as 3 attackers v 2 defenders. Or you can nominate two sets of two defenders and they alternate for so many times each.

The attackers may not pass back or introduce a scissors move. All passes must be towards the open side of each play.

The first attacker is the ball carrier and he MUST hold his line close to the two cones (the touchline) to hold the defence in. If he drifts across, the defence will win.

The second attacker runs as wide as he can to draw the second defender.

The third attacker comes between 1 and 2.

There are various potential scenarios and the players have to look up and watch the shape of the defence.

If the first defender does not stay on the first attacker, the latter just runs through to score.

If the second defender goes wide to the third attacker, the second attacker shoots into the space and calls for the pass.

If the second defender stays on the second attacker, the outside third attacker calls for the ball.

The practice is simplicity itself but it contains so many elements that all players need. The first attacker's role becomes the hardest for many players and it is worth persevering with it as it affects backs in full flight and forwards in handling in cramped conditions.

DIAGRAM 3

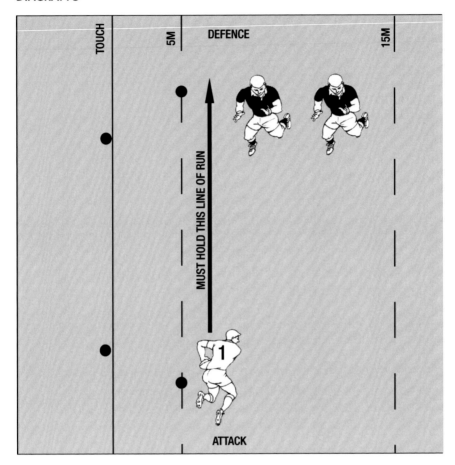

The defenders can play two-hand touch rules, but you can eventually make it live tackling in tackle suits when that becomes appropriate. Don't be afraid to place a couple of players at the end of the practice (facing the attackers) and ask them to report on why an attempt succeeded or failed; this reinforces the coaching message very quickly and avoids the whinge that "the coach is always getting at me." There is nothing like a bit of peer appraisal to show that you might just be right.

Once the players appreciate the skills, you can get the defenders to defend in different ways. They could defend with the outside player up first, they could scissors then defend or they could both target one player. One thing you, as coach, should ask them to do occasionally is *not* to defend. They could aim at space or simply both run to the outside attacker at the same time. You will be surprised how many attacking players will not see this, even though it is happening before their very eyes – and this translates into poor decision making in matches because the ball carrier has not appreciated what the defence is up to. So condition your players to play what they see in front of them; if there is no defender, run straight and win the war. If there is a defender, hold him in and pass to a support player. It sounds too simple to be true but it is a core part of the game that so many players simply cannot cope with, yet we churn out moves, ploys and complicated strategies when they haven't yet learned the ABC. If you need a simple doctrine, use **KIS** – **k**eep **i**t **s**imple; if you think you've cracked the coaching code, go one step further and employ **KISS** – **k**eep **i**t **s**eriously **s**imple!! Do not become tempted to paste over the cracks of skill deficiency with over-elaboration and moves. And if you have to have strike/set moves, practise aborting in the middle if it is not going to plan or a better option presents itself. A called move does not mean that it has to be followed through to the end – it is merely an indication of where you want to go if the opposition agree to the script.

If players really struggle with running straight, they will not be on their own. Running onto a pass and 'cutting' the ball (**Diagram 4**) is easy to talk

DIAGRAM 4

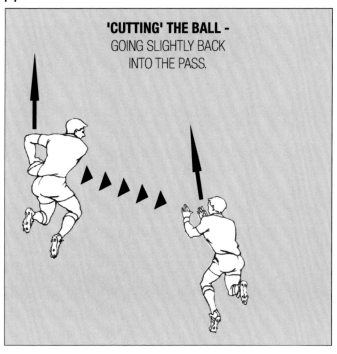

'CUTTING' THE BALL -
GOING SLIGHTLY BACK
INTO THE PASS.

about but it is not a natural action. It needs practice and one way to develop the skill is to use poles.

DIAGRAM 5

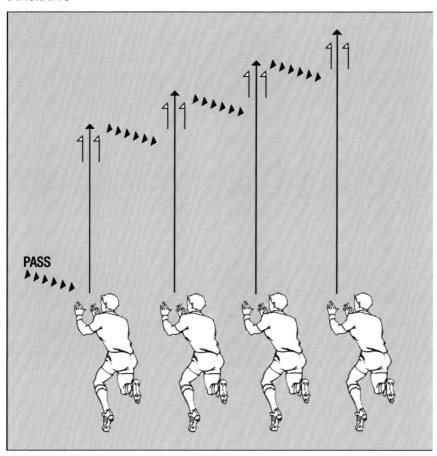

The players simply run through their space between two poles after receiving the pass and this stops them from running laterally across the pitch where they merely make life easy for the defence.

The coach can then start to put some pressure on by decreasing the forward space that the players have between sets of poles by decreasing the distance available to pass/take a pass. Do invest in plastic poles that have a foot piece at the base to allow them to be easily forced into the ground, so that you do not end up wasting time in trying to force a plastic pole that bends before doing what you want. If the weather has been dry and hot, very often in pre-season, invest in a lump hammer and metal bar as even plastic poles with foot assistance often seem not to want to be pushed into rock-hard pitches.

A further progression is to try to get the players to understand the concept of 'cutting' the ball as it arrives to hand. To do this, add another pole to each set of two.

DIAGRAM 6

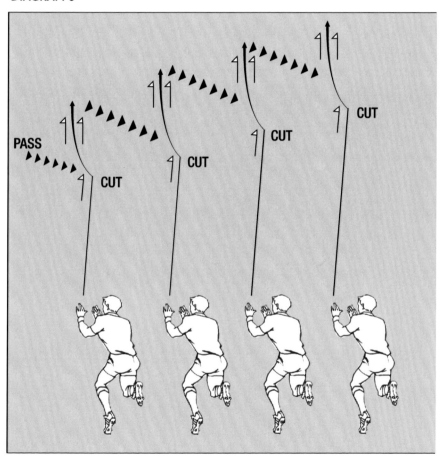

Each player has to run outside the new pole, then he has to cut back on a line into the pass and the space. This starts to replicate one of the most difficult skills in the game – taking a space and the ball at the same time. Most players get a pass then look for a space to run into. However, this is easy meat for a defender. It is far harder to defend a player who takes the pass just as he changes his line of run to hit a space, because the would-be tackler is initially being kept on the wrong line and a late change can force him off balance.

The player who takes the pass by 'cutting' the ball still has the option of an outside break after the 'cut', but he may find that his first 'cutting' line takes him inside the immediate defender and into space. And even if the defender manages to tackle, he is likely to be tackling on his weaker side on the inside arm/shoulder.

This aspect of play will not come naturally to all players and it is well worth explaining to them what happens when they master the skill. Show them (by walking through) how a defender has a strong side and a weak one in a passing movement. This does not occur so often among forwards who are supporting in numbers behind the ball, but it does affect backs every time they start to pass the ball.

DIAGRAM 7

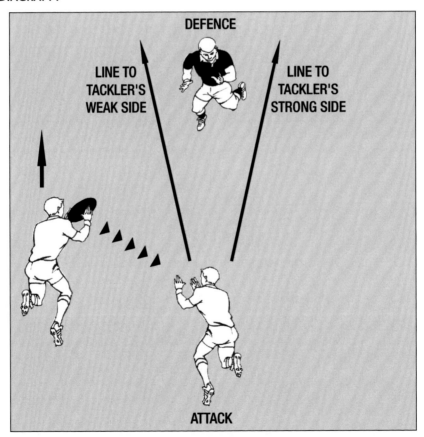

Once you get into the season, you might get a shock at just how much time you spend on organisation and fire-fighting at your two nights of training. When you are young and innocent, there are dreams of an hour and a half of dazzling skill practice, but dreams soon turn to the reality of the next league match. You will have injured players and you will be forced to compromise, whether it be to play somebody out of position or to bring the second team player straight in. In normal life, you bring the reserve player in, but this is not normal life and the second team player will never have what you really want; let's be honest here – if he did have it, he would not be in the seconds. And the injury rarely occurs to a player where a bit of a re-jig can suffice for a week. Why doesn't it happen to a winger or a blindside flanker? It has to be scrum half, fly half, hooker, place kicker or your middle jumper.

In the pre-season sessions you will have to have a fitness element and that will probably have to go on through the season as your players are unlikely to work out on rugby-specific fitness in their spare time. That is what training nights are for – for them, anyway.

You can go for an occasional 'mindless bash' approach and do not dismiss this out of hand; such a session, if used sparingly and at the right time can have a positive effect on a team when they know that it is deserved and necessary.

But there are various skill practices that can hold fitness elements while skill reproduction stays at a premium. There are countless variations that the thinking coach will be able to develop, but this is an example of running and passing under pressure that will test the players' hands and their stamina – just what occurs in match situations.

DIAGRAM 8

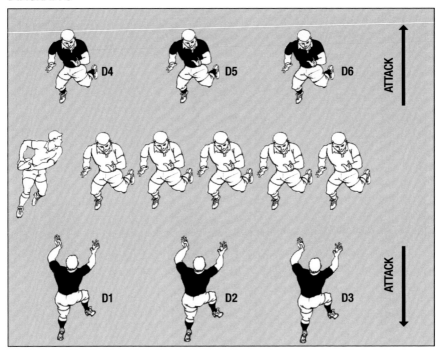

The practice is 6 attackers v 3 defenders and 3 defenders and is played on an area 30m wide and 22m long.

The 6 attackers alternately attack 1, 2 and 3 then 4, 5 and 6 – and keep going for a minute.

Defenders may come forward to pressurise the attackers but when the attack 'scores', they must retire to their goal line until the next wave of attackers starts to approach.

After 1 minute, the teams have 10 seconds to take up new attack/defence positions and the practice starts again.

Running this five times per team is probably a realistic aim for the first attempt and this can be increased as the coach thinks appropriate.

Use of martial arts' techniques. There are also various ways in which you can condition your players in the pre-season phase without using a ball and these techniques can easily be carried on through the season. We can learn a great deal from boxing, wrestling and judo and some of their skills and techniques can translate effortlessly to contact in rugby.

The first 'steal' would have to be skipping, much used over many years in boxing. It develops fast feet, co-ordination and cardiovascular fitness and costs virtually nothing. You can soon get your players to use this as a very effective warm-up technique and once they start to compete with each other, anything is possible.

There is a lot to be said for punching a hand-held tackle shield. The aim should be to develop very short periods of short, sharp punches and players very quickly start to improve their feet position and body shape for effective contact. This exercise can be timed so that you work the players in these short, sharp bursts of activity but the hands *must* be protected. You can buy lightweight practice gloves and they are well worth the expense, because bare-knuckle hitting against the tackle shield will certainly result in torn skin on the knuckles. If that is too expensive, try old towelling – but you must use some form of hand protection.

Judo has many elements that are useful to any player in the manipulation of his own and the opponent's body weight and balance. There is almost certainly a judo club near you and you might be able to find a friendly and willing instructor to take a few pre-season sessions on grappling, throwing and falling techniques. However, safety could be an issue so make sure that you get somebody who is used to controlling learners in groups – especially competitive rugby players.

The martial art that looks the easiest to introduce is wrestling. The rugby-related faults that you, the coach, might identify in wrestling will probably be related to balance during contact: feet too close together; feet too wide apart; over-extension of the body; centre of gravity too high; extending the centre of gravity beyond the balance base; crossing the legs; failure to modify the feet and body position; and losing concentration.

These exercises need the minimum of equipment but you do need to watch closely to ensure that your players stick to the rules of engagement that you give them. You can do without a skill practice that degenerates into a fight, so keep your eyes and ears open. If you have any injured players and/or other coaches, spread them out to 'referee' what is bound to become quite competitive and sometimes heated.

PARTNER DRILLS – WRESTLING TECHNIQUES

A. PUSH/RESIST

Partners number themselves one and two then place their hands on each other's shoulders.

PHOTO 1

On your command, number one pushes number two.

Partner two resists the push by constantly adjusting and modifying his stance.

Push/resist for timed periods of 15-30 seconds and change roles after each period.

B. PUSH/RESIST

As in A, except that the working partner attempts to push his partner into the ground.

C. PUSH/PULL/RESIST

As in A, except that the working partner attempts to pull his partner to the ground.

D. WRESTLE/RESIST

Partners grasp each other in a wrestling stance.

PHOTO 2

On your command, both partners attempt to wrestle/push/pull the opponent to the ground.

Both wrestlers constantly adjust and modify their stance.

E. SUMO WRESTLING

Partners face each other 1 metre apart.

On your command, both partners attempt to push/pull the opponent outside a 3 metre diameter ring that can be marked with cones.

The loser is the first out of the ring or the first to touch the ground in the ring with any part of the body other than the feet.

F. SUMO WRESTLING WITH BALL

One partner holds a ball and partners face each other in the ring.

On your command, the ball holder tries to stay in the circle and maintain balance while the other partner attempts to break his balance and push/pull him out of the ring.

PARTNER DRILLS (ON GROUND)

G. ROLL OVER

Partner one lies on his belly on the ground.

Partner two kneels beside him.

PHOTO 3

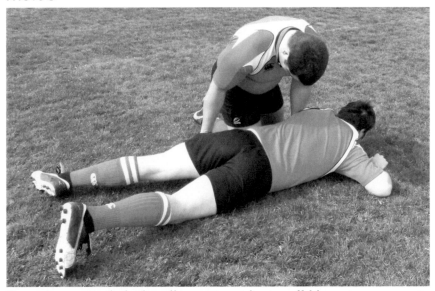

On your command, the kneeling partner tries to roll his partner over onto his back.

Partner one resists by constantly adjusting his body position.

Partner two must remain on his knees all the time.

The drill can be modified later by starting partner one on his hands and knees.

H. HOLD DOWN

Partner one lies on the ground on his back (or belly, or hands and knees).

Partner two kneels beside his partner.

On your command partner one attempts to get to his feet while partner two attempts   to hold him in his starting position.

Partner two must remain on his knees at all times.

All of this wrestling work is extremely physically demanding so you need to be very careful regarding the length of each repetition. You can achieve total fatigue, especially in the players' arms, in a very short period – so beware. You may leave them in such a state that they cannot carry out the next part of the session. Try to keep a record of how long they worked in previous sessions so that you achieve a balance and you can gradually build up the amount of time spent on each activity.

Other sports can also add an extra dimension to your team's fitness and skills. In the pre-season period and during some of the winter when the weather stops you training outside, it could be worthwhile contacting a nearby netball and/or basketball coach to run some sessions. Handling is key to these two games but there are far wider benefits. Soft hands, sympathy of pass, jumping to give and take the ball and different defences all make players more aware – and a session of man-to-man marking will turn the strongest legs to jelly. You have to 'think outside the box' at times when you consider what will add something to your training regime; it does not have to be rugby all the time.

As coach, you are on the horns of a dilemma with how much fitness work you should be doing at training sessions. You can run through your moves ad infinitum till the players can produce them at will – on the training paddock. But if those same players are unfit, the moves will never get past the first stages of production when the enemy start tackling and the red mist hits unfit players. There is a delicate balancing act to be maintained in your sessions and experience is almost all you have to find the answers.

In pre-season you ought to consider emphasising the art of low running with an effective and strong body shape. This does not come naturally, but if it is neglected you soon regret not spending time on it. New Zealanders have traditionally been the masters of 'spine in line' and the mantra is easily ridiculed but hard to disprove. Effective body angles are paramount at the scrum, the tackle, driving, rucking, mauling and taking the ball into contact; get ineffectively high and the game crumbles. Probably the easiest way to concentrate on this aspect of the game is to have short periods for all players where they use a net to get low body height. However, there is little to be gained by having the occasional session; you have to do a little bit regularly and try to get the net lower as players improve.

You will find a number of your players suffer from poor mobility, which can be the main restraining factor in failure to achieve a lower body position. This then means that you have to introduce mobility work to your sessions and your already limited time will be eroded with remedial work. Only you can solve this one and you will simply have to make a judgement on the weighting of the content of your sessions. I would suggest that each warm-up ought to have a stretching element and this should start at pre-season and carry on throughout the playing season – before training and matches. You will probably need some assistance in this area of expertise and the physiotherapist will be fine if you do not have a fitness assistant. But be prepared to rein in anybody else's commendable enthusiasm as they will be looking at mobility through professional spectacles and your spectacles just want to identify glaring weaknesses that can be remedied without losing too much time on the rugby part of your sessions. In the ideal world the players could have a long stretching session each week and they would carry on the process in their own time; you will not be in the ideal world and your players will, in all probability, just want a game on Saturday.

At some stage in each session you really will need a conditioned game – or part/aspects of a game. This is a minefield because you have to use the second team to play against and they will see such a session as a licence to kill (or maim or injure). So you, the coach, have to get a level of opposition that is appropriate to your team's needs. You can be reasonable and explain to the second team players what you want and remind them that they will get their chance to attack, but your team will merely do to the seconds what has just been done to them. You may as well accept that you will lose any argument based on logic, reason and common sense, decrease the numbers of defenders and load them up with protective tackle suits. Start at the end on this one – containing the warlike hordes is usually a doomed concept, so minimise their potential for causing mayhem and more club injury by decreasing the numbers of defenders and ensure that they wear tackle suits.

However, do you really need full-on fifteen v whatever? You might achieve more with a very simple skill/fitness game like this.

DIAGRAM 9

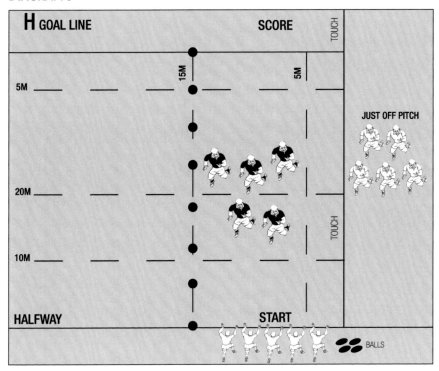

Split your squad into 3 groups of 5 in teams A, B and C.

Team A attacks, B defends and C rests. They change their role after each timed period of activity and in three periods, each team attacks, defends and rests.

The defenders can start by defending as they see fit, though you may have to adapt that if they stop too much continuity and you can arrange for 2 up and 3 back, or 3 up and 2 back – even 5 stations of 1 defender. Do not allow any defender to move backwards after he has defended – he is out of the game.

Place 4 balls at the start.

The attackers can only play one ball at any time and as soon as they score, all attackers have to come back to the starting line to collect the next ball

They have to score with all four balls before change of roles and if there is a sloppy or forward pass, or a ball is lost in contact, that ball has to go back to the start and does not count in that sequence of four. Be aware that you may occasionally have to help the attackers to score four times as their skills may dip as fatigue sets in and you may choose to overlook the occasional misdemeanour to help them.

The defenders are allowed only to tackle and defend – they may not try to win the ball. The coach may have to condition how many players the defenders are getting to the tackle so that the attack gets some success.

This little game practises many elements of the game while working on fitness levels. You will coach lines of running, drawing a defender, passing, contact and offload skills and basic tackling and body position for the tacklers.

You might decide to allow kicking – seeing and utilising the space behind the defence if the defence is tight, in the attack's face or winning the confrontations.

The coach must referee and coach at the same time – and players need to communicate, something that does not come easily to our players after the best part of a playing lifetime at school being told to shut up.

Encourage this communication during all practice sessions and games. You are not looking for noise; what you require is information being passed between players and if they do not practise it at training, it will probably be overlooked during Saturday's eighty minutes.

Passing out of contact is one of the game's most important skills that can so easily alter things very quickly, but it has to be introduced well before the season begins If an attacking team is simply going into contact time after time, the defence gets used to soaking up any impetus and the attack usually loses possession or patience or both. The pass just before or just from contact can be devastating as the tackler is out of the game and the next defender simply cannot get to the breach, especially if the receiver of the pass from contact runs a little J line, which takes him close to the original tackle.

DIAGRAM 10

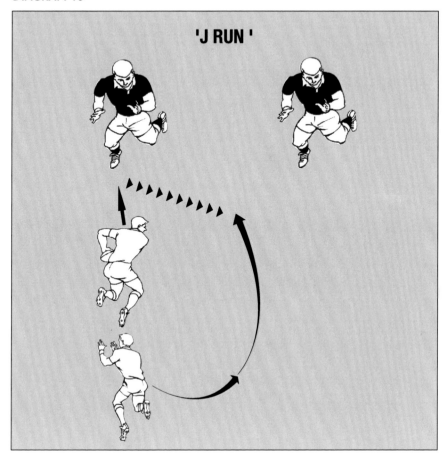

However, the pass from contact's effectiveness is virtually nullified if the support runners are too flat on the ball carrier. As soon as the ball carrier is held, the flat support runners automatically run past him, so the pass is not a serious option. The key is to maintain depth in support, but this is very difficult to define; it is a bit like trying to explain how long a piece of string is. Players will always ask what 'deep enough' means and you can best help them with two bits of advice as answers: if you think you are too deep, you are probably about right; and you should be able to read the number on the ball carrier's back – and if he has not got a number, deep enough to read it if there were one there.

Once the pass from contact is an option, the pass must be soft. Too often the pass is fired at the receiver, thus making his mind up for him regarding where he can go. If the pass is soft and slightly lifted, the runner can decide which space he wants to hit and he, not the passer, should make that decision.

There are so many ways to practise passing out of contact and in the end it has to be done with a live tackle. You can run through with a group v1, v1, v1 and so on, but the ball carrier has to be comfortable with what he is doing as he takes the contact and you must stress that there is no need to rush the process. If the offload is not possible, the tackle should be taken and the ball placed on the ground for the support to deal with.

There can be a number of options in when the pass is given. (1) The pass can be given just before contact so that the tackler is committed and out of any immediate further play. (2) As the tackled player is falling behind the tackler and (3) When the tackled player actually hits the ground and passes from the ground. Whatever does happen, the pass is best given with both hands as it is very simple for the ball to be knocked out of a one-hand carry. Few players have hands that are large enough to control the ball with one hand.

DIAGRAM 11

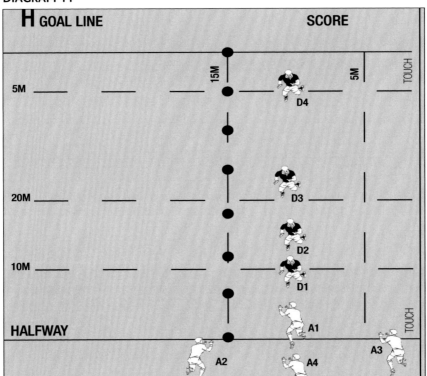

A useful practice can be used to suggest to players that rarely are they too far from the ball for the offload option. Some think that they have to be directly and immediately behind the ball carrier, but this is not so. The time it takes for the tackled player to start falling or to hit the floor allows support to be effective from quite a distance away.

Work between the 5m and 15m lines.

Use tackle suits for all defenders.

A1 goes into contact rom D1 and the three support players have to make a decision (and communicate it) regarding who takes the offload.

The receiver will usually be A2 or A3, but if they overrun the contact A4 has to mop up and it will usually be from a pass off the ground.

Whoever takes the ball has to become A1 and go into the next contact while the other three attackers reorganise into A2, A3 and A4.

No support runner may go early and must wait till the contact actually starts before he goes for the offload pass.

The coach must 'referee' the process, especially when players will instinctively want to go early to get the pass. The coaching message must be that there is usually more time available than you think and a late run can be a devastating one on the defence.

Tackling and its importance cannot be over-estimated, though I would not subscribe to the view that tackling wins games. Tackling allows teams the *opportunity to win games*, but you have to score points to win – and I have yet to see a tackle score a try, penalty or drop goal.

A side that relishes tackling can gain not only turnovers, but also the psychological edge in a close match. If the process of the tackling is sound with good technique *and* there is a bit of bite and urgency in each contact, the defenders will gain the upper hand if all else is equal.

On top of any tackling carried out in your training sessions, do try to get your players used to practising tackling *after* every session as well. Put them in pairs and have one carrying a ball from a couple of yards from the tackler. It does not have to be done at any pace, but the tackler should end up on top of the ball-carrier then stand up as quickly as possible and rip the ball from him by squatting down to him rather than bending over. Get each player to perform, say, ten tackles each. It does not take long, but it reinforces the importance of the skill if you keep coming back to it. Make sure, however, that each tackler practises equally with each shoulder as players will select their stronger side if they are allowed to. The practice also ensures that players see the tackle as not always a solitary and isolated skill; if you have the chance, you can get up quickly and 'steal' the ball before any of the opposition support can arrive.

In any tackle practice, do not let the players dive into the tackle. Coach them to keep running as long as possible and launch into the contact from close-up. Diving is spectacular but should be reserved only for when the would-be tackler has lost his man and last-minute heroics are called for. Some of your players may have been coached in their formative years to dive; it is up to you to re-educate them to keep running into and through the tackle.

A useful coaching tip for your players is to suggest that they look slightly beyond the target rather than at it. This has the effect of making the tackler raise his head slightly, thus keeping the spine straight and strong in the tackle, which minimises the danger of injury. If the head is allowed to drop, the tackler is not in a strong, dynamic position and the thrust into the tackle will be lost because of a curved spine. Such a weak position also hugely increases the possibility of injury.

Insist on shoulder contact from the tackler at all times and do not allow arm tackles in training. In a match, an arm tackle may be all the tackler can produce but it is weak and allows the attacker to break through it relatively easily. Even if the arm has to touch first, coach the player to keep running through that touch so that his shoulder eventually makes contact. The tackler can then dominate the collision, thus reducing the options that the tackled player has.

CHAPTER 4

ASPECTS OF THE GAME TO CONSIDER BEFORE MATCHES START

(a) Importance of the place kicker in the game. The importance of a goal kicker cannot be exaggerated in rugby union. In the ideal world you would probably have him as first choice on any team sheet – then a second one as reserve in case the first choice is having a bad day at the office. Penalties and conversions are the easiest, least tiring and unopposed method of scoring in the game– and nobody can tackle the kicker!

The drop kick is also a useful way to score so find out who is best at it and do not fall into the trap of assuming he has the number ten on his back. You will need strategies and plans to ensure that you get the ball in the right place at the right time during a game – and that the designated kicker is ready and in the right spot. The whole team needs to know what is being planned so that they are aware of precisely where and how the appropriate possession will be available.

But don't leave it all till match day. Make the drop kicker practise against a couple of defenders at training sessions and get them to attempt charge-downs. It is as well to have at least one attacking centre alongside the kicker in this practice as there is a very good case to abort the drop kick attempt if one or more of the defenders gets too close to the ball. They are virtually out of the game in this phase and it can be a productive moment for the kicker to do no more than attract the intended charge-down and give a pass to the first available player, who ought to be able to find a space to attack.

Then there is the unplanned drop kick, which has to be encouraged if you have a player with good technique. Even if the attempt fails, a chase can be very dangerous to the defenders. Such a chase ought to be part of penalty kick attempts, because too many teams stand and watch the attempted three point effort. Organise a chase of at least three players in case the kick falls short or bounces back from the post or crossbar.

Kicking is a skill that tends to belong in the category of 'he did it last year' so most teams go along with that. Why not, however, find out for yourself who is good at it? Hold some tests and competitions pre-season to sort out who can kick in a reliable method – and regularly. Success here does not automatically mean that the kickers who seem to be effective and in control of technique will be able to perform when the two league points are hanging over them like the Sword of Damocles, but you will get pointers before the season starts.

Do not assume that your kicker has to be from the backs, but do resist most forwards' entreaties to be considered for the role. They tend to be capable of prodigious feats at 6.45 p.m. on Thursday, but that is not a very reliable guide to their likely success rate seventy nine minutes into Saturday's relegation or promotion battle. However, if you have a forward who is reliable and accurate under match conditions, use him.

Make sure that your two kickers practise in a sensible manner. They do not need to go for length – the process of accuracy with a *constant* kicking method is what they should aim for. Get this aspect of the game right and you will never regret it.

(b) Simplify the options that your players really do have when they are running with the ball. Don't be afraid to go through a checklist with them and you can build up a pecking order of what you want them to do. You are, hopefully, de-cluttering their brains by simplifying the available options. This may smack of regimentation but on occasions it can be useful in this complex game. This list of options does not *have* to be followed – you can easily rewrite it to suit your team's requirements.

(i) **Beat the man** in front of you with a sidestep or swerve. We don't practise this enough with the whole team, especially with the big forwards. When a large object is driving at an opponent, the tackler will almost always slow down and sink to prepare for the impact. That is when he is extremely vulnerable to a change of direction by the ball carrier and the forwards especially can surprise themselves with how (relatively) simple it can be – probably because it has not been suggested to them before.

A useful warm-up session can easily use this practice that needs no more width than 6-7 metres.

DIAGRAM 12

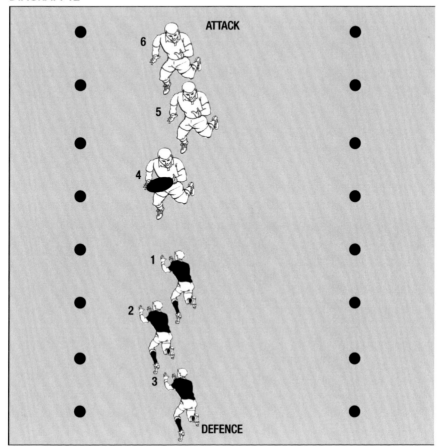

It works like a continuous relay.

Player 1 passes or kicks to 4.

4 tries to beat player 1 in the space available.

If 4 beats 1 he passes to 2, who passes or kicks to 5 – and on it goes.

If a player is tackled or is pushed into touch, he passes to the next player in line to keep the sequence going.

The coach controls how much/little contact is acceptable at the tackle. It can be two-handed touch or a proper tackle. However, if a full tackle is allowed, it is best to restrict it to below the waist to avoid potential unnecessary injury.

(ii) **Pass** to a support runner to beat the immediate defender, a skill that you will practise at all sessions.

(iii) **Pass out of contact.**

(iv) If the ball carrier is held, the next attacking support player (whatever his playing position) hits the ball to **rip and pass**. Whenever this happens the ball carrier is responsible for presenting the ball at an effective and appropriate height to bring the support player in low. This is the ball carrier's responsibility – even at the drive from a lineout. Too many attempted drives end up going upwards because the ball was initially held too high. The 'ripping' effect from the second player isolates the ball from the defenders; if a maul has to be set up, the ball is not at the contact point, but is safely at least one player back from that point and even if the maul is collapsed, the ball is still relatively easy to play backwards from hand.

If the rip and pass is not on, the second player who latches on to the ball should keep his legs pumping to keep forward momentum. A **driving maul** can be set up and this can ultimately offer excellent possession for a passing attack.

If a driving maul is the option, the second man (first support player) must not be held in his original position by the next group of support. They must go beyond him and drive on the original ball carrier, allowing the first support player with the ball to drop back to the rear of the maul, where he is now in control of the movement and the options.

Do not allow any more hands near the ball as you want stability and certainty in this phase. Too many hands add to the chance of a handling error. When the maul begins, get the players to concentrate on short, sharp steps when they try to get into what should be the scrummaging position and try to encourage talking so that information is passed between the players in that maul.

(vi) The player is **tackled to the floor** and he passes (two-handed) when on the ground.

(vii) If the ball cannot be passed safely from the ground, then the **pick and go** by a support player is now a serious option and you can again simplify the decision making of what to do. If the backs call for it, that call should override all others and you must have a one-word command for this. It has to be shouted so that the forwards know that they are just winning the ball. However, if there is no signal and the pick and go is considered, coach a simple technique to help the forwards. If the player picking up to go can make at least a couple of steps with the ball without an opponent to tackle him, it is probably a good decision. If defenders are closely and immediately in the way, it will probably not be productive.

(viii) If there is no space for the pick and go, **pick up the ball and feed** to a support runner.

(ix) If opponents are too close and the pick-up is dangerous, **clean out or protect** the possession. If the clean out is required, put in as many forwards as are required to keep the ball.

Contact skills are made much easier if you have effective ball carriers. It is not a bad template to get at least one ball carrier in each of the three rows of the scrum, though professional sides would want more. However, they have the time and money to develop or simply buy what they want; you are likely to have to make the best of what is available.

(c) **First man to the tackle hits the ball with lead elbow and shoulder before it goes to ground** – whatever his position. If the ball carrier is held up by the opposition, you cannot have a situation where the backs wait for the forwards to do the dirty bits. You will find that many collisions occur in the middle of the pitch and the centres will be closest. Encourage the backs to go in for the ball if they are closest to it – it can produce early ball. A key element of success is *not* to use the fingers at the first contact as the hands are a relatively weak starting point when elbow and shoulder initiate more power.

The initial ball carrier must take the responsibility of setting the height of this first contact and must work hard to present the ball at a height that can bring the next player in at an effective height. If the ball is held too high, the next player in will lose most of his momentum because he will be too tall; make him come in low in a powerful manner.

In your coaching, always make the players aware of the fact that valuable time can be saved if they practise watching the ball carrier's body language. Too often you see a player go into contact *then* the support players react. However, the ball carrier always sends visible signals regarding which shoulder he will lead with. Well before the contact takes place, the ball carrier will start to adjust his body position and one shoulder will nearly always start to drop before the hit. That is the moment when the aware support players can steal a priceless split second and know where the ball is going to be presented well before the defender gets in. The support players can also guess whether the ball is going to be up or down and if it looks as if it will be up, the first support player should aim to latch on to the ball before the contact/tackle. This ensures that you claim the ball, the defender will not dominate possession and the ball can be played just on or just before the contact occurs. It is not a long process in time, but it can produce effective 'early' ball. Practise it and reinforce the coaching message whenever you can in training; once players train with the concept, they will start to do it on the pitch during matches.

(d) **Back to 1.** This is an aspect of the game that I have found to be crucial. Players have to learn that a call or signal does not mean that the called move or play *will* happen; it is hoped that it will, given the right circumstances.

Even the briefest period of time in any game of rugby at any level requires some complex stringing together of a series of fallible skills – and opponents are trying to tackle and generally muck things up. Even a 'simple' passing movement can be fraught with problems and all players need to practise when they put an end to a sequence and **go back to 1.** It might be a simple decision to take contact instead of giving a hospital pass, but it could just as easily be a back row move being nipped in the bud as the ball is coming out of the scrum in the wrong place or the scrum has been wheeled. These are decisions that have to be respected and it is not always a fault to tuck the ball up the jumper and drive it on when a spectacular move had been called but looks doomed pretty soon after the call.

Do try to get this important concept across to the players without them all screaming, "Back to one" whenever they happen to get the ball. It will, if appreciated and understood, save silly points being given away because they carried on with something that had the kiss of death about it. If your team is going through a wobbly period, they may need the reassurance of winning the ball simply and driving it on through the forwards before a box kick is used to get the side running forwards again. Sometimes a 'simple' long kick can lift the forwards if they are flagging and fighting a losing battle, so preach the message that 'back to 1' has a place in any team's vocabulary.

(e) **Play what you see** is a very simple instruction to give to players and in the ideal world that should be the foundation of any successful team. But how do you, the coach, know what the players see at any given time? Do all the players, or even a few, see the same thing? And if they do, will they all get their reaction to fit the ball carrier's actions?

It is a complex area, so be very careful before you ask your players to play with what you think is a precise instruction of 'play what you see'; it can be extremely imprecise. The majority of your squad are likely to have learned the game from coaches who had little insight into the game and relied on packages of drills; these coaches and drills may have conditioned players' reflexes to hunt for contact. But try to start the re-education process by being more precise and specific than asking players to play what they see. Why not start by asking them to scan for spaces and to attack them? You might have to offer some simple 'rules' such as the first receiver, usually the fly half from the scrum half pass, *must* 'cut' the ball and he *must* hold that line back against his opposite number's inside shoulder. However, he may be forced to run across with the pass, so again a simple little 'rule' could be that if and when this occurs, an outside player must exaggerate a cutting line to try to straighten up the possession.

You have to have the confidence to coach attacking play where the players learn (in some cases this means unlearning years of previous habits) what you, the coach and fellow players mean by 'play what you see'. The more opposed attacking you can practise the better - and video will be very useful so that you can discuss the options taken with the players after the session. This can be done after match videos as well, but you have to get across to the players that you are questioning to assist, not to criticise. Some players get very tetchy when their decision- making is questioned.

A fairly simple method of coaching the concept is to tell defenders what to do at practice. Get them to do odd things, so that the attackers really do have to play what they see. You can get some strange results, for example, when you instruct all the defenders to fall down at a certain point in the attack; the results can be hilarious because too many players will be playing a move well ahead of where they are and many will pass even when all of the defenders are lying down – so they are hardly playing what is realistically in front of them. The top international players will be comfortable with the 'play what you see' attitude, but even they get it very badly wrong and occasionally miss what look like simple scoring opportunities.

So devise practices and strategies to help your players. Talk to them about options and win their confidence with encouragement rather than condemnation when it does not go perfectly to plan. But there is no single drill or practice that will give you this on a plate; you have to develop and nurture it and make your side comfortable in the awareness that any player can be responsible for decision-making.

One very simple decision-making practice, which can easily be refined and/ or modified is to set up 4 attackers against 4 bags and 3 defenders.

DIAGRAM 13

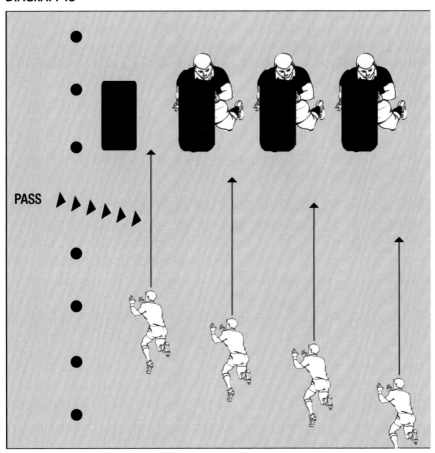

A scrum half passes to the first receiver and the defenders move sideways into either gap available on the coach's instruction. The coach can call one, two, three or no defenders in any combination that he requires, but there will always be a space to attack. If all the spaces between the bags are defended, the ball should go to the last man who scores. However, if a defender does not take up a space, the attack should spot that and go through the space to score. The coach can make this progressively harder for the attack by calling the defenders fractionally later each time, which will force the attackers to make quicker decisions. (If this practice proves too difficult, go to 3 bags, 3 attackers and 2 defenders – then go back to the starting point of 4 bags at a later stage.)

(f) **Backs' moves or not?** This is a thorny problem but you can do a lot of good work pre-season by *not* talking about moves for the backs. You will no doubt develop some and they will, in all probability, not be new; they need be no less effective for that.

Once you agree that certain moves will be used, do walk through them a few times with the whole team so that everybody can picture the move before it is used at full speed. This is especially important for 6,7 and 8, who will probably be the next players to link or pick up the pieces from the tackle if and when it occurs.

Different players learn differently and some will never visualise a move from a blackboard diagram, even though they think they 'see' it. Play safe and walk everything till the whole team can visualise the components of the play.

However, there are two things that you can do before you settle on any moves to give the backs the edge.

(i) Run games of touch as suggested earlier and encourage the backs to run dummy and decoy runners from all phases of possession. You and they will be amazed at the confusion in the defence that can be caused by this simplest of strategies, but it requires hard work from the runners and the decoys must never see themselves as decoys as they should be decoys who may just get the ball – so their lines of run must suggest that they could get a pass. If they run outrageous lines that would never get a pass in the next hundred years, how can they expect to draw defenders?

Once they get into 'decoy running mode' you can discuss what works best and there will be common themes that you can utilise in your game plan and moves. The strength of any decisions will be that the players have had input. You may develop or find a move that contains the elements of what you have discussed. Use it – even if it is a well-used move, the players themselves will have almost chosen it because of their observations.

(ii) Amaze your wingers and tell them that they will, from now on, run for most of each and every game. Wingers are an odd species but they can be very lazy if they can get away with it. They will now become the centre of just about all you do in attack – and it is simple. Generally, you will see the blindside winger watching the rest of the backs when the ball is spread to the open side – and some wonder why overlaps are hard to create.

(g) Your blindside winger must make himself available as a runner at all times and probably outside your fly half.

DIAGRAM 14

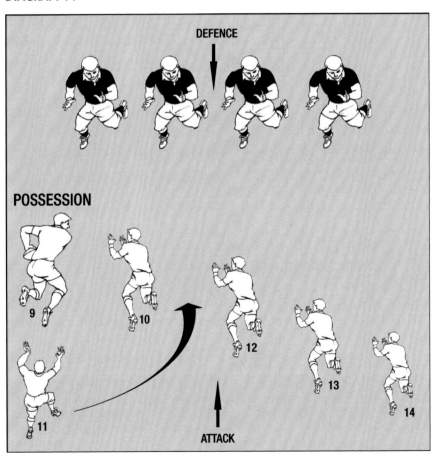

If the fly half runs an effective holding line to hold in the defending 10 and open side flanker, the defending 12 has a big decision – what to do about the attacking blindside winger. If the defending 12 stays on his own man, the blindside winger can take a short ball from the attacking fly half. However, if the defending 12 comes back to take the attacking blindside winger, a space must appear in the place he has just come from and a pass from your 10 to your 12 should put your 12 in space. You may think this is over-simplified, but I assure you that it will pay dividends, especially if your attacking blindside winger goes late. The tendency is to go too soon so that the defence can see exactly what is happening and they simply move their own blindside winger to nullify the extra man. If, however, your winger delays till, say, the lineout ball is in the air or the ball is in the scrum, he will be pleasantly surprised at how many opponents switch off and fail to cover his run infield.

Once the blind-side winger is working in this manner, the full back can then pose a threat with his incursion and the defence becomes overloaded as they see more players moving than they are usually accustomed to seeing.

A very important part of getting success with any handling process is to condition all players to run with both hands available at any time they may have to take a pass. It sounds simple and probably is, but too often support runners run quickly by driving both arms. This does not allow that player to present a target for the passer, so it is hardly surprising that the passer often has to guess where the target is likely to be. Far better for the support to show both hands with the fingers up in a W shape **PHOTOGRAPH 4** at the point where the pass needs to end up.

PHOTO 4

The receiver should also stretch the hands towards where the pass is coming from. **PHOTO 4a** This is beneficial in that (1) the pass is not in the air longer than it would be if the hands were held in front of the receiver's body and (2) the pass means that the receiver can take then give in one clean, uninterrupted movement. If the ball is taken in front of the body, there has to be a movement (i) back towards where the ball came from then (ii) the pass. It is a slicker pass from the hands that are presented towards the passer – and it saves time that can be valuable in a split-second decision situation.

PHOTO 4a

This goes for forwards supporting from depth just as it does for backs in a threequarter handling movement. Practise and coach the presentation of a W target for all players so that it becomes the norm when they are likely to get a pass.

The passer then has to offer the ball in a sympathetic manner and it should not be hurled at the receiver. This will not happen just by talking about it; it is a vital core skill and should be emphasised and stressed at all practice sessions. You might develop skill practices to get the point across, but I'd suggest that it should come into *each and every* practice, drill or run-through that you do. If the importance is always stressed, the players will eventually respond because it will be at the front of their 'must do' list when they are passing and/or receiving.

It is then imperative that the pass goes in front of the receiver, not at him. This, of course, means that the support has to start from depth so that there can be a pass in front; if he starts flat with the passer, it becomes virtually impossible unless the passer can produce early forward momentum to create depth. Away from the top level, it is safer to get the depth into the equation without the man in possession being responsible for creating depth for the next support runner.

If you develop some strike moves, ensure that the whole team knows the calls and get them shouted out loudly. Valuable split seconds can be gained if your support players, especially the forwards, know where they are meant to run. If the scrum half wishes, he can give clear instructions to the forwards in the same way as they will be given for where kick is going. Split the width of the pitch into four, 1, 2, 3 and 4 **DIAG 15** and convey the area that is to be attacked with the intended/nominated carrying player's number and the area that he will be aiming for. Thus,

13 2 when you are winning the ball on the left suggests that the outside centre will be cutting back to the left of the posts or towards the left post.

12 4 when winning the ball from the right side shows that the first centre will be heading for the right-hand section of the pitch.

As in all aspects of the game, make sure that the players adapt to circumstances when things do not go to plan. You tend not to win many games when too many players hurtle willy-nilly to where the ball was *supposed* to end up. The call to show where the ball is going is just an initial guide; it may have to change as circumstances alter and players must practise to understand that and adapt to what actually unfolds.

DIAGRAM 15

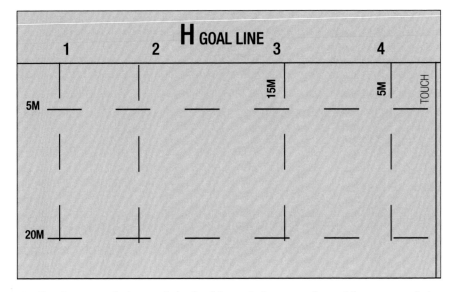

(h) **Ruck v maul.** A good deal of hot air is wasted on this aspect of the game as many contact situations leave the tackled player with no option. If you are flattened after receiving a bad pass, you will probably end up on the floor as you did not enjoy the luxury of any time to stay on your feet to form a maul. Then there is the teeny-weeny semantic aspect, such as 'when did you last see a ruck?' The ruck has been replaced with clean-outs with one or two players, so the real dilemma is whether you want to play from ball up or ball down when you have an option.

When you consider this, just ask how many options are available to your team when the ball is down and an offside line has been created, allowing the opposition to set their defensive line. The options are few; pick and go is a good one if there is space or you might pass to the outside players or even clean out the opponents and then pass the ball. There is not a lot left in the way of choices.

The ball-up scenario, however, allows all sorts of realistic options and it is difficult for the defence to know precisely what is going to happen and when. The immediate response should be for the next player to the ball carrier to hit the ball to safeguard possession and all sorts of potential attacking options can begin. He can twist the ball out and feed a runner, a driving maul can be set up, decoy runners can start to buzz from a new ball carrier – all of which might just perplex the defence if carried out with conviction and speed. If it all grinds to a halt, you can set up and feed the 9 for a kick. Generally it is a win-win situation.

But the really big benefit from ball-up is the speed of it. It is so much faster than a ball on the ground that has to be cleaned-out before getting back into circulation. If you need to convince yourself and/or the players of this, set up a practice where two groups of players simultaneously run through a ball-up and a ball-down practice side by side. The ball-up will always win the race if the next man to the ball carrier does his job properly and hits the ball just as, or just before, the defender comes into contact. The group that uses a 'hit the ball' technique before the contact is completed should nearly always be valuable seconds ahead of the team that goes to ground and cleans-out.

(i) One skill well worth practising is **getting strong in contact**. Too many players lead with one shoulder and hold onto the ball with both hands, but this is so easy for the defence – all they have to do is lean on the ball carrier and he will go to ground. Coach the ball carrier to grab in behind the defender with his lead arm while shielding the ball in the rear arm. This makes the ball carrier very strong and, unless he decides to go down, he is virtually impossible to tackle to the ground. Of course this is little use when he is tackled round the legs and has to go to ground, but practise the options from a grapple that does not take the legs away. A decent mantra is 'fight to stay on your feet.' Then you can take that a stage further to 'fight to stay on the pitch' and don't let the defender dominate – unless, of course, it suits your team's purpose at that stage of the game to be forced into touch.

Once the ball carrier grasps his opponent and would-be tackler, he can keep the legs pumping and the defence can quickly be in disarray if that drive gets into their heart, as they will have to run backwards and then through the gate if a ruck or maul ensues. And this is where you might consider a method of recycling the ball that is not at all common – but it works. If the ball carrier has driven and has to go to ground, the normal shape of his body goes across the pitch **PHOTO 5a** However, a far more dynamic and urgent action is for the ball carrier not to go across the pitch but to keep his legs pumping then hit the ground horizontally and long to the length of the pitch **PHOTO 5b.** This really can scatter the defence and it offers the ball carrying team the chance of really early ball when the defence is still retreating. If the players who are cleaning or picking and going play this appropriately, they can be in space and behind the defence in next to no

PHOTO 5a

PHOTO 5b

time. Give it some thought – it may be a play that can get you clear and into space before the opponents know what is happening and it is dynamic.

When the ball is on the ground you may have one player who can take possession before the opposition arrives in any numbers. In all probability, though, you may have to commit two or more players to clean out the opposition and your leading pair must bind tight as they clean out. Not only does the bind make them a more compact and powerful unit, but they offer a more effective target for any other players coming in to assist. If they bind loosely, **PHOTO 6** any player coming in and onto them will probably hit the backside of one of them and spin him out away from the target of the ball. If the two are binding tightly from the start, this is less likely to happen and the ruck/clean-out will have a greater chance of success.

PHOTO 6

In any tackle scenario where the tackled player is going to ground and he cannot offload, he must place the ball only after hitting the floor. It is a precarious situation if he tries to 'plant' the ball when the rest of his body is moving and will lead to imprecision and a possible turnover. He must also 'plant' with both hands so that the ball goes exactly where your team wants it; a ball held in one hand is easily knocked so that the ball spills badly.

If the defence is swarming all over the tackled player who is trying to 'plant' the ball, he has two realistic options so that it is as difficult as possible for the defence.

Players normally place the ball close to the body. **PHOTO 7.** They must get used to placing the ball as far backwards as possible so that the defender has to lean so far across the tackled body that he ends up in a weak and unstable position. **PHOTO 8**

PHOTO 7

PHOTO 8

Place then roll the ball backwards in a controlled manner, but be aware that once the ball rolls back more than a metre it is outside the tackle zone and is available for any opponent whether he has come through the gate or not. It must not be a wild fling – the possession must be available for the scrum half when he is slightly in the clear from traffic.

When you do win the ball at ruck or maul, watch closely how your half backs play next. There is a tendency for the scrum half to send out a long pass, but this can defeat the object of what you are trying to achieve as your team will be biting into valuable outside space. Try to encourage your players to hold the defence in with a short pass from the scrum-half and the next receiver can simply run straight if the defenders are not in place; a short pass from this phase with effective running lines can pay dividends.

(j) **Fast ball**. Why on earth does any coach want fast ball? Fast ball can be seen at most poor games, so be precise with players and coach the philosophy of **early ball**. I could come along to your club and get your team to give me fast ball in seconds. All you have to do is slap the lineout ball and let the scrum possession fly out, then you simply hurl the tackled ball backwards and, hey presto, you have fast ball. This is a cop-out; insist on quality possession and preach early ball.

A useful tip for coaches is to stand in the defensive line in practice and 'feel' when the attack has an advantage. There is a short period when the attack holds all the cards and the defence is retreating or is on its heels. If 'going through the phases' creeps in, however, the defence quickly gets onto the front foot even though the opposition is winning and recycling possession from the contact. Players have to be aware of the crucial differences in the state of readiness of the defence; if they are retreating or on the back foot, that is the optimum moment to run the ball at them. Spectators will never see or understand this and you have to be on the field to 'feel' it.

So, if the defence is on the back foot or retreating, get into them with ball in hand. If they are on the front foot, you have to develop some strategy to get them going back. It may be that you have to kick and this can be very useful and advantageous as the defence will take longer than usual to retreat if they started on the front foot. They then have to turn and get back to the new action area.

(k) **Pods**. Forget them! They are a legitimate term in the lineout where you will have various pods of three players in a jumper and two lifters, but whoever first 'invented' this concept in loose play has a great deal to answer for, especially lower down the rugby food chain. Two pods actually happen naturally and may be all you need. At a scrum when the ball goes right, the right prop, right lock, right flanker and No 8 will get away; at the scrum where the ball goes left, the left prop, left lock, left flanker and No 8 will do it; at the full lineout the thrower, jumper and two lifters will be occupied, thus leaving the other forwards as the first pod.

Unfortunately, once you define those pods, some, or all, of the second group think that they only go in when it is their turn when they should, in fact, go in if needed; and all of the first pod think that their job is to go in at the first contact even if and when they are not needed. So you frequently end up with too many of the first pod going in and not enough of the second. Result – you lose the ball – unless the opposing team is as rigid as yours in interpreting the coach's instructions.

It is far better to refrain from being too specific on pod numbers, accepting that the first natural split will probably occur at 4/4, or not far off that Thereafter, the players surely have to be available as needed, otherwise you will simply not win loose ball. It has to be a hugely efficient machine to operate 4/4 pods throughout various phases and that efficiency will be very hard to find away from the professional scene.

The coaching mantra should be along the lines of "Go in if you are needed - or if you can make a difference."

(l) **Only run early ball when the backs can go forward** and into space. If the possession is slow and the defence is on the front foot and dangerously close to your back line, you have to have a 'Plan B' to regain the initiative of forward momentum. The simplest answer is to stand the fly half slightly deeper than he would be if he were running the ball, then bring in a kick of some description; the bomb, a dink behind the flat defence or a long kick to a space are decent options. However, a running strategy is not always out of the question. That strategy might be something like a Rangi **DIAG 16** or a

DIAGRAM 16

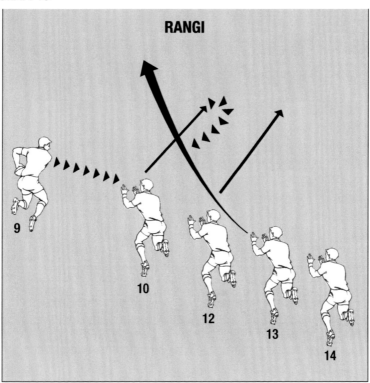

RANGI

DIAGRAM 17

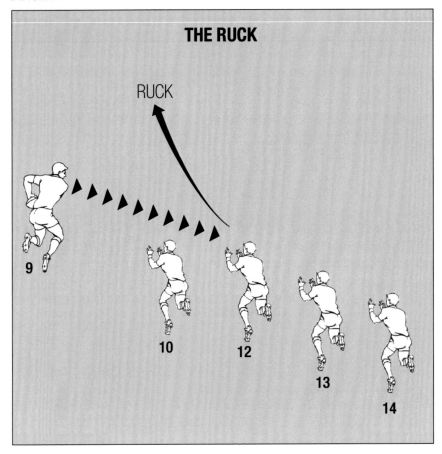

short ball straight to the first centre followed by a quick ruck **DIAG 17,** but I have always favoured the blindside in these circumstances. It is relatively safe for handling and if you can get two passes in you are probably going to make a lot of ground. Failing that and the ball is slow, you have to have a kicking policy mentioned at the start of the paragraph to get your team going forward again.

(m) **Blindside principles**. The first thing to achieve is not to pass too long to eat into the space, which is already limited because it is the blindside. Avoid miss passes and too many fancy bits – get your blindside attackers to run hard and straight; two passes will wreak havoc in the defence.

It is an area of the attacking field that is largely underused, yet defences can be very vulnerable there as they tend to concentrate on the bigger picture of the openside. This alone makes it worthy of consideration and if you do take the ball there, the defence will not be able to overload their openside defence on the next occasion.

It is a particularly useful area if your possession starts to slow down. You might consider kicking slow ball, which would make sense. However, get your fly half to shoot to the blindside from slowing possession at the breakdown and this injection of pace and a pass (or two) can beat opponents – or at least get them on the back foot while you restart the process of winning early ball. A trundling, predictable pattern of harmless 'hits up' into the openside will not have the same impact as a quick transfer to running into the blindside.

(n) **Confuse opponents** – consider 'outrageous' plans to make them think. Make a great show, say, of putting your ugliest flanker at 10 or 12 – then don't actually use him and pass across him. However, you must practise with him being asked to be more than a decoy player as the ball may just go to him and it is too late for him (and the rest of the team) to moan "But I haven't practised this!"

This is only one example of the sort of subterfuge that can be developed. Whatever you do, draw opponents' attention to it as you will not gain any advantage if the opponents are rugby brain dead and do not realise that you have started to carry out a play; to be honest if they are that dull, you may as well not try anything out of the ordinary against them.

Watch any coach working with his players and you will invariably witness a strange sight, though it doesn't always hit you immediately between the eyes. He will almost always practise with passing from left to right. There is no logic, yet we all fall into that trap and players, through their playing careers, will have had an imbalance in the way they have been through drills and practices. Check out what you do and put it right if you too have been a predominantly 'left to righter'. Just be aware that you need to change sides frequently in practice – be self-vigilant and try to get a balance as your players will generally have to pass right to left for about half of the game time on Saturdays.

However, if many coaches do maintain an imbalance in favour of left to right practice, why not capitalise on it? That team in opposition will probably be less proficient in the game from right to left so have your first long kicking option going left. They will then have to pass from their right to left to get out of trouble and may not have a left-footed kicker who can produce a good wiper kick from the right to left movement. That means that they may have to have a right-footed wiper but, while not too difficult (the kicker just stays a bit deeper as he takes the ball), it does take a bit longer and the slight advantage is still with you. If he has to stand deeper, you can then blitz his attempt and really put the pressure on him.

CHAPTER 5

DEFENCE

Defence is not the same as tackling, though you generally have to have people who will tackle (or at least look like they will) to defend. There are many important aspects of defence before you decide which system suits your players. The coach needs to develop a team's attitude to defence where they take a pride in not letting the opposition past and they will have to be comfortable with confrontation. There is a need to go-forward in defence just as much as when you attack and enthusiasm to work in an aggressive unit will pay dividends.

The attitude that a coach should try to engender is one of total commitment within the defensive structure and pattern. Most players become more determined as they get closer to defending their own goal line and all too often this evaporates as they get closer to what they see as safety on the half way mark. It is vital that they are encouraged to develop the 'five metre attitude' over the whole pitch so that solid and dynamic defending is good everywhere.

In any defensive system there has to be good communication, so that everybody involved knows what is going on and players must practise changing their collective mind in the middle of a play.

Most importantly, however, is discipline within your strategy and in the way it is refereed. There is little point in practising what you think is perfection if you get penalised for it. The players must be prepared to adapt to suit what the official requires, even if you and they think he is wrong.

Your players will no doubt watch televised matches and they will be hugely impressed with the outside-up, or banana, defence. This involves the defence starting with the openside winger going up first, followed by the outside centre then the inside centre. **DIAGRAM 18**

The outside defender (D4-14) comes up quickest and the speed decreases slightly to (D1-10). All defenders cut back slightly so that they tackle with the inside shoulder (right shoulder in this example). It is a very intimidating ploy and the early ball carriers can be tackled in possession when they look up and see the outside defenders ahead of where they usually are.

DIAGRAM 18

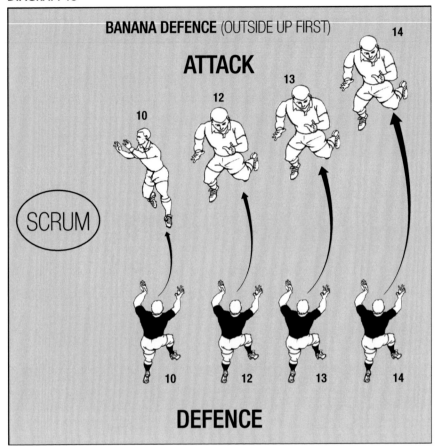

BANANA DEFENCE (OUTSIDE UP FIRST)

ATTACK

DEFENCE

It puts enormous pressure on attackers, particularly in wet and/or windy weather and they have to stay deep to get their passes in, which can allow the defence to tackle behind where the ball was won.

However, if the defensive line loses its shape, or one player is up too quickly, inside spaces are easily available for the ball carrier. It is also vulnerable to a grubber or 'dink' behind the defensive line.

On balance, this might be one to leave out of the repertoire as it does require a great deal of time to perfect it – and your referee may penalise you for it *looking* offside.

My advice would be to start your club with one of three far simpler defensive systems (or a mix of all three in different situations):

'Up and out' defence, usually referred to as **drift** or **slide** defence and/or

'Up and in' defence, usually referred to as the **blitz**.

'Up and hold.'

(a) Up and out – the drift.

DIAGRAM 19

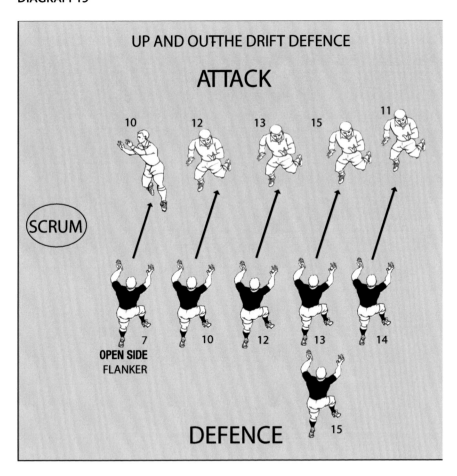

The tacklers start by moving towards the inside shoulder of their opposite number. Once their first man passes, the slide can be called so that the first tackler can then slide towards the second attacker, thus forcing the attack to move laterally and run out of space. If the defence works well, the attackers will find that they are moving uncomfortably and ineffectively towards the touchline.

There are dangers with this system, not least if any defender moves sideways before the ball leaves the attacker's hands. There has to be a very clear call so show the rest that the ball has definitely been passed and the push can start.

There is also vulnerability if the attack has a player who can bring his next outside player flat on the inside (weak) shoulder of a defender. You will need a covering defender, which could be the scrum-half, to track across and backwards just inside the ball so there is insurance against a line break or a chip through.

The first two defenders in the drift should keep pushing sideways into their next outside space just beyond the attacker that they were marking but *only after their man has passed the ball* and they must keep inside the new ball carrier. This has a good chance of nullifying any inside pass or switch.

It is a small point, but think carefully before you use the word 'drift' to your players as the word implies laziness and a casual approach – things you do not want. Perhaps you would avoid the subliminal message of drifting and call it 'push' when any communication is made.

(b) Up and in – the blitz.

DIAGRAM 20

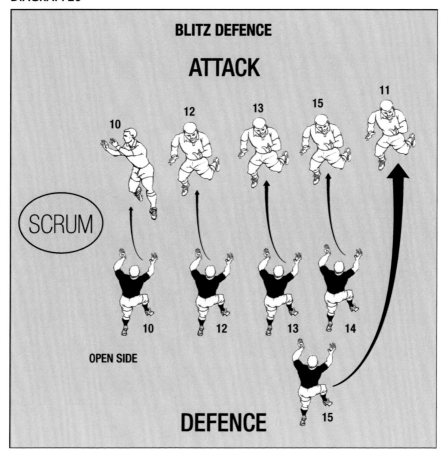

The defenders start by standing a bit wider and on the outside shoulder of their opponent and initiate an aggressive and fast advance to push the attack back infield. There is an element of risk but the attack has to have good handling skills to beat it as they are deprived of time and space very quickly. If the weather is windy and/or wet, this can be extremely effective.

(c) 'Up and hold.'

DIAGRAM 21

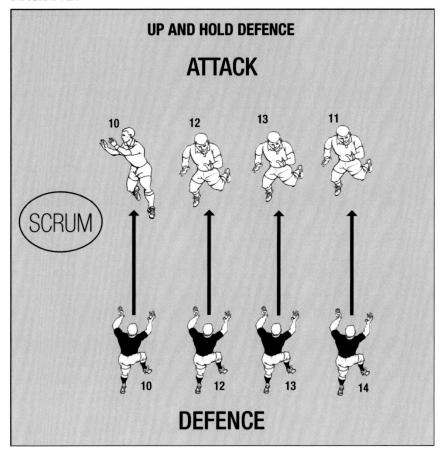

This form of defence is not as aggressive and 'in your face' as the blitz defence. Defenders move together and move up flat against their opposite number to show a wall of defenders to the attackers.

The system must have a line of defenders who move up together with confidence as they have to move at the same speed and hold their line, whatever happens in front of them with dummy runners and decoys. If a single player fails to stay with the common pace, the inevitable dog-leg appears and that immediately becomes a weakness that can be exploited by the attack.

The coach must consider what his players are capable of and choose a system, probably in consultation with the team, which is achievable. Avoid over-complication and try to simplify the options that your team will consider when defending. Do not be fooled into thinking that it will work effectively because a team did it in a televised game; they practise for hours and have the most able personnel available.

If you are coaching tackling, defence, or both, do coach players not to watch the ball being carried. They should work on watching the attacker's hips and feet so that they know where to aim; a ball being waved about should be of no interest.

A very important rule in defending, whichever system you use, is *not* follow the attacking team man-for-man before they have won the ball. They might start from a scrum by overloading one side or another. The chances are that they are simply trying to get you to cover them with the same numbers so that you have left an imbalance on the other side – and guess where they are going! In such situations mark space, even if there is nobody there when you first line up. The fact that you have a balanced defence will almost certainly stop them from going through with their initial plan.

You will decide which system suits your team best, but do spend time on the cover defence to track the ball in case the first line of defence is breached. This will probably mean that you organise a combination of No 8 and scrum half, but it is a very important element of effective defending.

When the opposition get close to your line, the full back generally wants to defend in the middle of the backs; that is fine from a lineout where there is, until the ball has been played through at least one tackle, no blindside wing space. However, I have always thought that the blindside is the most vulnerable area for any defence and have always advocated a simple rule: the closer the opposition get to the line from scrum, ruck and maul, the more blind-side the full back covers. If they are five metres out with a wide-ish blindside, he has to be in there. If they are twenty metres out, then he can afford the luxury of standing, say, between the centres. But he should be very aware at all times that the attack may hit the blind – and he has to get to it!

The back three must always work **together** to leave two back in defence. If the opponents handle towards your right winger, the left winger must track across and back to create a back two with the full back; if they are going in the opposite direction, your right winger works across and back with the full back to form a back two.

DIAGRAM 22

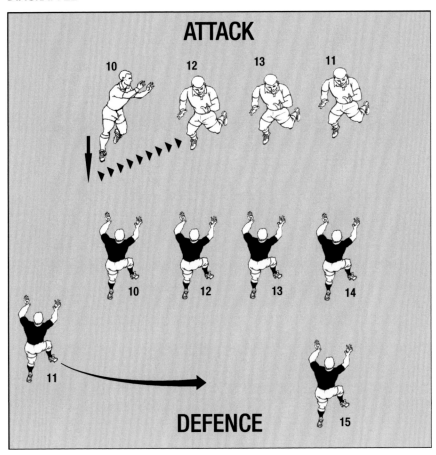

There is no simple answer to who covers what when the attacking full back enters the line. There are arguments on both sides between (i) defending full back takes his opposite number or (ii) he lets his own winger come in to take the attacking full back and he stays out on the attacking winger. I favour the simpler answer of full back on full back, leaving the winger to cover his opposite number. Wingers generally have the pace needed to take another winger and he will be playing opposite him for the whole game and should know some of his strengths and weaknesses.

There is no hard and fast rule that dictates what you decide to use, but your system must be practised with first and second squads so that any player moving up knows what is going on. It is not a bad idea to insist that all the club's teams follow what you do, even if other coaches may not be totally in agreement; it is up to you to convince them and let them know that the committee of one, you, has made the decision.

CHAPTER 6

GETTING OUT OF TROUBLE WITH A KICKING POLICY AND HOW TO ATTACK WITH KICKS

Once you have spent long hours in formulating a kicking policy, wait for a while before you let your players know what it is and check that you have the people with the kicking skills to carry it (or parts of it) out. There is little point in impressing your team with your vast well of knowledge on how to use kicks if the kicking personnel are thin on the ground, non existent or plain useless.

Once you decide that you do have the kicker(s) that you need, it is very important that they practise in a structured way. It seems very simple to suggest that you will go long at a certain point in a game, but the appointed kicker needs to be pretty certain that the skill he is about to perform has been used a few times in the previous week's and weeks' training. Too often a kick is a last resort when all other reasonable options have disappeared; the kick is then the last chance saloon scenario and that explains why it is often cobbled together and ends up unsuccessfully. The trouble is that it looks so easy when the players impress each other on training nights before the hard work begins. Props preen and display awesome leg power in propelling the ball to all areas of the globe, but they are unlikely to have the opportunity in the league match on Saturday.

You can organise some basic structures that will be relatively straightforward. But I stress, the kick needs practice and the follow-up or chase must be a regular chore for the whole team. You must not see strategic kicking as a one-man job; the other fourteen have a duty to know exactly what is expected of them and it generally requires running fast after an instant response to the kick. However, they cannot afford to neglect precise instructions on who stays well back as a safety precaution if the opponents decide to whack it straight back to you. You will need a policy and it will almost certainly require two players who have a decent return kick from hand, so consider leaving back some combination of full back, winger(s) and fly half.

You may have only one or perhaps two kickers who can reliably kick long, so try to ensure that one or both do not chase a long kick in case the opponents immediately kick back long to you. Get another player to work hard to get behind the initial kicker before the ball is kicked so that he can then chase the kick from an onside position and work other players onside who were initially in front of the kicker

And if you have a kicking plan or policy, it is a good idea to let the rest of the team, especially the forwards, know what is about to happen. There are all sorts of ways to achieve this, but you need to keep it simple and you could do worse than have a signal with the player's number followed by a position on the pitch where the kick will go (or might go, in some cases).

You have already split the pitch into four areas (based on the width of the pitch) to signal where the ball is likely to go from a called move in the backs (See page xxxx). The numbers are exactly the same for kicking , 1, 2, 3 and 4. You just start the signal with the letter K, showing a kick, then add a number for the area of the pitch you will be aiming for.

K 9 4 – a box kick from scrum-half on the right side of the pitch.

K 10 2 - a bomb from the fly half after possession on the left side.

K 12 4 – a wiper from the centre after possession on the left.

When you use the box kick, it must be seen as a means of regaining possession and not just a ploy to relieve pressure. It is nearly always carried out on the right, but is perfectly acceptable if the scrum half is left footed and/or can get the precision on the left.

The first requirement is to get height on the ball and not to send it too far. Your chasing winger should then jump for the ball and try to catch it. If his opponent catches it, he should be tackled and preferably into touch. There should be a pincers movement with a flanker, usually the openside, coming into the ball as well. Then a centre ought to sprint behind their would-be catcher in case he aimlessly taps the ball back. See **DIAG 23.** You do not have to follow this formula slavishly and a centre could be part of the pincers with the 7 going behind where the kick lands.

However, do coach your scrum half and winger to watch closely what is happening. If their defending winger is well back, why box kick to him? Just pass to your own winger and let him run into an unguarded area, which will be far more productive than kicking to a man who is already back there and waiting for the ball.

DIAGRAM 23

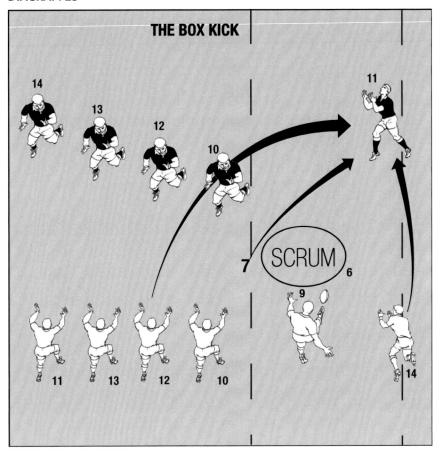

There is a useful game that can be run by the players themselves – and kicking is key to success. Play on a full pitch with 3 v 3 and it is a good idea to play your back 3 players against three others – 3 of the same team backs or perhaps the back 3 from the seconds. There can be a very useful discipline and fitness aspect to the game as well.

Start the game with a drop kick restart from the 22.

From then on, whoever receives the ball has to kick it from where he received and controlled it.

The choice of kick is entirely at each player's discretion and the aim is eventually to get to a spot from which a drop or place kick can be employed to score three points.

If the defenders catch the ball before it bounces, they get two kicks, the second of which may be an attempt at goal.

If the kicker kicks straight out, the opposition get possession from where he kicked – unless he kicked from the 22 restart and the possession is taken from where the ball went out.

When a kick is being taken, the other two players must get back behind the kicker (fitness and discipline elements).

The kicking team may not challenge for the ball once they have completed their kick.

Once a score is made or the ball crosses the dead-ball line, the game is restarted from the 22 with a drop kick. If the catchers catch a failed attempt at goal they have two kicks starting on the goal line. If the failed attempt crosses the dead-ball line, the game restarts from the 22 with a drop kick.

You can change the restart points to suit what you want. The numbers of players can be whatever you want them to be.

The game does make players very aware of where spaces are and where the defenders are standing and puts a premium on kicking to space rather than to opponents.

CHAPTER 7

SCRUM AND BACK ROW MOVES

One of the biggest problems with back row moves is that the forwards tend to think too far ahead and fail to win decent primary possession. Instead of worrying about the next important job, which might be no more than getting a strong bind and good hit, a few in the pack start thinking of the break, the scrum half take and full back coming into the move. It often ends in disaster.

The essence of any successful planned back row move is the quality of the initial possession. Once that is won, then the forwards can start to think of their next most important task, which should usually be maintaining the pressure on the opposition to make it harder for them to get their own back row off to defend. A nudge up from the prop on the side the move is going helps a lot as it allows a bit more space to work in for the attack, takes their first defending flanker and no 8 slightly away from the move and allows the attacking No 8 to run forwards right from the pick-up.

However, if the attack's tight head prop comes backwards and the No 8 still attempts to pick up and go to the right, the move is almost certainly doomed because (i) the No 8 who picks up has to run backwards before he can go forwards and (ii) the defending flanker on the side of the attack will have been turned close to the No 8 who has picked up, making his defending duties relatively simple.

DIAGRAM 24

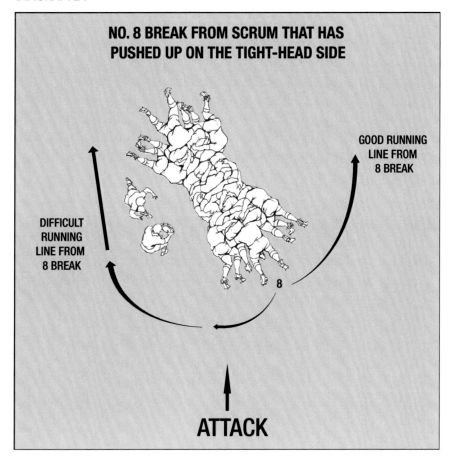

NO. 8 BREAK FROM SCRUM THAT HAS PUSHED UP ON THE TIGHT-HEAD SIDE

GOOD RUNNING
LINE FROM
8 BREAK

DIFFICULT
RUNNING
LINE FROM
8 BREAK

8

ATTACK

Much the same is true for a less common back row attack going left. If the loose head prop comes backwards, the move left is going to be very difficult and should, in all probability, be cancelled if the scrum does wheel the 'wrong' way.

Once the players understand the importance of any wheel at a scrum, you do not want the intended ball carrier (usually No 8) merely laying his hands on the scrum and that is as far as his effort goes – then he wonders why he does not get the big stage to show off his break from the base. It is far better if he goes in and pushes immediately with both shoulders, though he will not necessarily agree with this analysis. A break from a pushing no 8 can be far more dynamic than one from a scrum with only seven working forwards

– and his pushing presence minimises the chances of the defending scrum going for an eight-man and pushing the attacking scrum off the ball.

An element of the game that requires constant attention is getting the initial 'hit' right so that you are on the front foot at scrum time. It defies logic that the lawmakers came up with the word 'Engage' to take the forwards in. The word has two syllables, so when do you start? I recommend that you practise by considering the word as 'En' and forget the 'gage' part; if your pack waits for the full word from the referee, they will never get the vital inches of advantage at the first impact and it will, in all probability, end up as a poor scrum engagement.

Whenever you plan a scrummaging session, do take simple precautions to take as much risk as possible out of the activity. Always start with a robust warm with 1v1, 2v2 and 3v3 to get the mind-set right. You cannot allow complacency and relaxation to come near the scrum practice! Then get the players into something like wrestling in a small space – it soon concentrates the mind and prepares them for the scrums.

If you are live with two packs, do not let them loose on full, eyes-out contact from the start; that is inviting trouble. Try to have a few scrums where the two packs go against each other without the full blast. Once they are comfortable and prepared, pump the level up a bit. However, in my experience, you might have to deflate it a bit when the seconds start to stake their claim for a first team place.

If you are working on a machine, do check it out each and every time you use it. Hit the pads yourself to check that the club joker has not put the pins in to stop the machine's heads moving; check that there are the right number of springs so that the heads do not move too far (or not at all!) forwards and especially check that there are enough springs to hold a fair bit of downward pressure.

Back row moves do not have to be complex, but they do work best from a rock-solid scrum. The following examples are easily performed and are hard to defend.

DIAGRAM 25

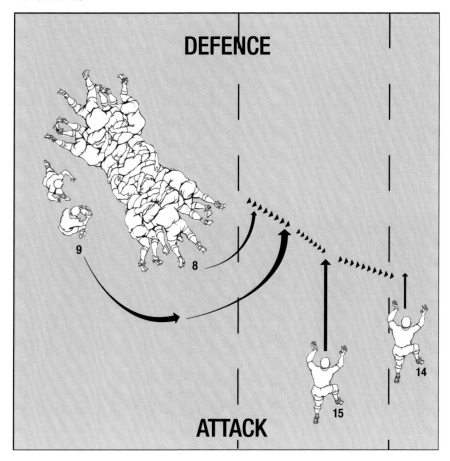

This is one of the oldest back-row moves in the game, yet it will still work when done well. When there is a decent blind side, the No 8 picks up, runs (not too far so that he is tackled) from the scrum that has preferably pushed up a little on the tight head side, passes to the scrum-half and the full back then times his run onto the pass and into a space with the right winger in support.

DIAGRAM 26

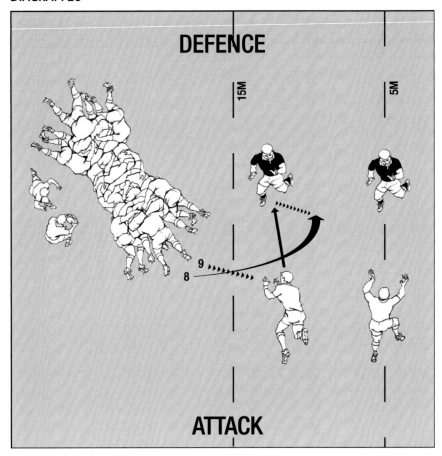

This move does not require as much blind side space on the right as the previous move. One of the centres moves into the blind side and takes a flat pass from the scrum-half. His first job is to look for a defender, aim for that defender's inside shoulder and leave two options. (i) If the defender stays off the tackle, the centre keeps running straight and past the defender, and (ii) if the defender comes into a tackle, the centre gives a circle-ball pass to the No8 who will then have his right wing in support with the extra option of the full back coming in.

At times, however, you can even work from a ball that does not get to the No 8 in the intended manner. Sometimes the ball comes out of the scrum at the side and the flanker can simply pick up, call his intentions and go. The rest of the pack can react to this, especially if you have practised the scenario at training. The opposition will probably not have a clue where the ball is so you ought to gain an element of surprise. Don't let your players expect everything to happen in an organised way as it might on the flip chart at a team meeting; practise the unexpected and capitalise on it.

You can also practise a move to the left side, which can surprise defenders as they expect you to go right from the back row move. When you have a narrow blindside on the left, try using a flip back from 8 to 9, who then feeds the left winger.

DIAGRAM 27

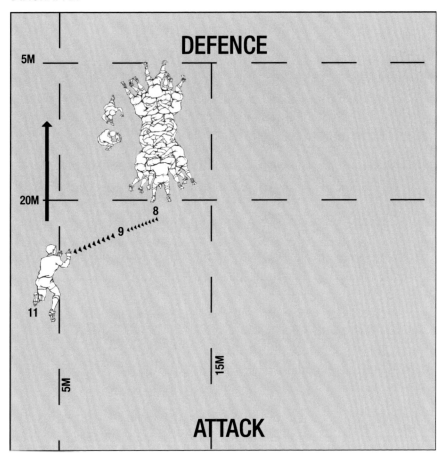

You will have your own methods of practising scrummaging and there is no doubt that practice will improve the effectiveness of any set-piece. However, do try not to fall into the trap of asking the forwards to push blindly against a machine till they drop. It is far more effective to tell them what you want before the session begins. Don't be afraid to put a realistic maximum on how many you want – and specify how many, say, on your put-in, the opposition put-in and so many eight-man, eyes-out gut-busters. You will get more from the players if they know what is expected.

We all try different techniques, but the firm bind, good body position and positive hit will never become redundant. I like all the pack to be on the front studs with the heel raised so that there is no laziness at the set-up stage. One of the best descriptions I ever heard was that all the pack at the scrum preparation should feel as if they are ready to dive into the pool at the start of a swimming race; they are just waiting for the starter to fire the gun. That sums it all up perfectly and gives the players a clear coaching picture where complex instructions might not be easily or readily taken on board.

One key element of scrummaging that is frequently overlooked in the quest for effective ball-winning is the importance of the stomach muscles – the **abdominals**. They are a vital aspect of core stability and are crucial in the weight-bearing exercise that is a scrum. It is usual to see players being reminded of the important back position, feet position and the angle of the head, but try to add the abdominals to their check list before engagement and you might be pleasantly surprised at the difference it can make when all eight of the pack tighten-up their midriff at the same time. If you watch quality weightlifting, the lifter will make a conscious effort to tighten up the core before the lift; try punching a punch bag without sucking-in the stomach and you will not hit effectively. This short process can become very important in your quest as a coach to improve your team; get all eight to tighten-up the abdominals just before the referee calls the engage.

The scrum machine is an important tool but is usually underused. Try to train your forwards to use the machine for a few minutes on individual work if they arrive early to training. There has to be a degree of supervision and common sense so they will be advised to work in pairs with one working and one supervising the exercise. The coach can work on all the forwards initially but you can soon get the key points across so that they can take some control later.

The springs have to be altered so that a single player can just about get the machine's single head to move forwards no more than about 23cm (9 inches); allow too much forward momentum and the benefits are nullified as the player will stretch too far onto nearly straight legs and you do not want that in any scrum or scrum practice.

Get the player to crouch and follow the referee's (fellow player's) verbal commands of "Crouch. Touch. Pause. Engage." Do not let the player stand too far away from the machine as he will want to 'win' the engagement with momentum; you want to develop power. When he hits, coach him to shuffle the feet forwards to 'follow the hit' so that he does not extend the legs, an action that leads to an ineffective scrummaging position. When the pads have been hit forward, do not let the player bounce straight back; he must hold the hit for a couple of seconds then he has to work through his core stability muscles to let the machine heads come back slowly and in a controlled manner.

This is an elementary form of resistance training and can be beneficial for all forwards, not just the front row. You can have two players hitting at any given time but the coach has to teach them what they are working on and what the spotters are looking for if spotters are being used. You must not allow too many springs to be discarded as too much movement forwards can be dangerous. The machine should be moved as soon as the ground condition deteriorates then the roller soon repairs the marks.

When individuals practise to improve their scrum technique, the difference can be marked when the eight come together and they all concentrate on the basics that they have practised individually. However, if they have practised individually on poor technique, the effort was wasted.

If you are not comfortable with coaching the scrum, be prepared to analyse body positions and don't be afraid to comment. The forwards, front row in particular, love to preach the myth that there are dark and dangerous secrets that only they understand, so take them on. The scrum is all about being together with a tight bind in what would be acceptable in weight-lifting technique. Look at a weight-lifter's position **PHOTO 9,** turn it around ninety degrees **PHOTO 10** and you are not far off what you want from the eight forwards. The feet are pointing forwards, not sideways, legs are at a maximum bend of half squat, the back is straight and the head is tilted slightly upwards, So when the fraternity of Stone Age men approach you

PHOTO 9

PHOTO 10

and suggest that they enjoy scrummaging with their feet in the ten to two o' clock position, right shoulder down and backside two feet above their spine, disabuse them of their ideas and try to get a degree of change. This, unfortunately, could be the impossible task, so stay sane and coach the next generation of props into some sensible and sound technique.

When the players have achieved a very tight bind it can become *too* effective and the second rowers cannot get their heads in between hooker and prop. **PHOTO 11** The simple answer to the problem is the wrong one as the props then tend to relax their grip to let the second row in, thus nullifying all the previous good work on the strong bind. There is a very simple remedy that maintains the bind yet allows the second row to get in.

PHOTO 11

The prop on the side of the entry problem (or both props at the same time if neither second row can get his head in the gap) must not move his hips or feet sideways away from the hooker to leave a space. He simply has to slightly rotate his foot nearest the hooker and rotate the heel away from the hooker. **PHOTO 12.** This means that the loose head prop moves his right foot slightly clockwise and the tight head moves his left foot anti-clockwise. The movement is hardly perceptible but it allows a second row entry while maintaining the shape and strength of the pack's tightness.

PHOTO 12

CHAPTER 8

LINEOUT

Once upon a time, long before lifting was legal, this phase of the game was reasonably straightforward, though not particularly productive. I still remember the days when there was a good deal of huffing and puffing, a great deal of skulduggery and very little ball coming back from the lineout. It used to resemble a battlefield and the Laws on lifting have certainly made it a more reliable means of possession than it ever was pre-lifting. Unfortunately, too many teams do not consider what they are doing and stick too rigidly to the status quo in the game.

For instance, where in the law book does it say that the hooker has to throw in and forwards have to jump? Yet we nearly always see the hooker throwing in and often badly. Surely the task should go to the player best suited to the skill demands, so if you have a player in any position who can become a reliable thrower-in, why not give him the job? He may be your fly half, but it is surely better to win the lineout without the 10 in place than it is to have him standing in the normal (correct) spot and all he has to do is tackle because you have (again) lost the lineout.

The same goes with jumping. It is all very well for professionals to lift an eighteen-stone behemoth – they are pumping iron during most of their waking hours. But the amateur ranks will soon run out of puff if they have to keep raising their eighteen stone lump from, if not the dead, something close to inertia. So try some new ploys. The lightest player in most teams is the scrum half and many 7s teams use him as the lineout ball winner; why not give it a go? Your lifters will be able to get him higher with less effort than it takes to get a second rower lower, so at least consider using any player so that you win the ball - and it does not have to be a forward just because that is what most other teams have always done.

When you know who your thrower-in is, look carefully at the way he throws and get him to practise basketball free shots to work the knees in the action. Too many throwers are leaden in all parts of the body apart from the arms and hands, yet the skill does require a soft push from the knees and up to get any sympathy on the throw.

Your thrower may be one of the imprecise band of brothers who uses only one hand in the throw. This rarely works and the ball all too frequently slips out sideways and you give the opponents an opportunity to have another lineout with their throw or their scrum for not straight. Try to get your thrower to adopt a two-handed action where he takes the ball behind the neck and guides it forwards with the non-throwing hand. When this is accompanied by a soft push from the knees, you will get far greater success and the thrower can legally hold back the throw with this action as he does not have to release as soon as the body and knees start to work. With the one-handed method, he almost has to release as soon as the arm moves. If, however, your thrower is reasonably accurate and cannot change from a one-handed throw, accept things as they are as you will probably try to mend something that is not yet broken. You will not have time to rebuild an action if you are in the middle of a league season and have a maximum of two nights of training. Be aware, though, that you will probably be developing younger players for the future, so try to influence their method and aim to copy the action of the best Premiership and international players; most use two hands, take the ball behind the neck and push sympathetically from the knees. They also happen to have worked extensively on their core stability in the abdominals, but you may not have sufficient time available to contemplate this.

If you have a serious lineout problem even after considering who throws and who jumps, you have to consider early calls and running to a throw-in that occurs as soon as the lineout is formed. This requires practice, but it can be very effective as most teams have developed conditioned reflexes at lineouts and they want to hold a mass meeting and discussion on what you might do. Beat them with speed. And there is absolutely nothing to stop you having a two-man lineout, which, when formed quickly on a call as the ball goes into touch, can easily disorientate opponents who are conditioned to assume that there *has* to be a lift. There is no such requirement in Law, so use that to your advantage.

You will, unfortunately, have to have the referee's support and it will be well worth a few minutes of his pre-match time when you check it out. Hopefully, he will go along with you and allow what is a perfectly legitimate ploy to speed the game up and get the ball back in play, but referees are human and can say one thing before the game and put a slightly different interpretation on what they previously said during actual play. If the quick lineout was plan B, you now need C.

Plan C is not to have lineouts at all whenever possible after the opposition kick to touch. Your back three players have to work really hard and get the ball back in play before the opposition arrive, but you have to be absolutely certain that you have the personnel to carry this out competently and at the right opportunity. There is little point in making a mess of it and giving the opponents possession without having to do anything to earn it, so bin the idea if your players do not have the pace and nous to succeed. They also need to know that they can take a quick throw as long as they use the match ball and it has not been touched by any other person after it went off the field of play.

Once again, this requires practice as the rest of the team need to know what is likely to happen next and they need to know where they are likely to be running, but it is well worth consideration if you know your set piece lineout will probably not win the ball. In training you need to look at various possible scenarios so that the back three players understand when *not* to go ahead. It is far better to lose a lineout than to attempt a quick throw when all the odds are stacked against it, such as when the kicking side has chased really well and they leave you with no space; make sure your flyers realise that they do not have to carry on with the ploy simply because you practised it on Thursday night. This can be a perfect practical illustration of 'back to 1.'

If your team is having lineout problems you will probably not win the opposition's throw-in, so your kicking policy has to take that into consideration and you should be trying to kick to space rather than to touch. However, you will never get a game where you can do precisely what you want, so your weak lineout will have to be worked on as soon as possible. If you are still struggling after carrying out various remedial practices, probably the best strategy on their throw-in is to jack a man up at two and put the rest of the forwards on a watching brief to spot if and when the opponents 'mess-up' their throw and/or catch. You will be surprised how much possession is available if only players are honed to look for it at and around the lineout – and that process starts at training nights.

Whatever you come up with, you, the coach, must not allow lifting on the shorts. Not only can this be extremely painful for the man being lifted but it is also a very poor lifting method as much of the dynamic of the lift is lost as the fabric of the shorts moves.

PHOTO 13

The correct grip is **PHOTO 14** and the main coaching point after that is that the two lifters should move together so that they are almost touching. This ensures that each lifter is working through a strong, vertical back (good weightlifting technique) and not through the arms alone **PHOTO 15,** which is a very weak lifting position and tires the lifters' arms out extremely quickly.

PHOTO 14

PHOTO 15

Once you have won the ball life does become relatively simple, but one skill that does not get the attention it deserves is the early ball off the top. Too often it is slapped back, which can be extremely imprecise and dangerous for the scrum half. Try to get your jumpers to practise 'stun and push' as the ball comes to them. They let the ball come into the hands and stun it for the briefest of moments before pushing to the recipient. The benefit is that the ball is controlled and there is no need for wild panic from a badly deflected or slapped ball; it also allows the jumper the opportunity to keep hold of that ball if that becomes necessary. Once he has slapped it away, a hold is not an option. Players might regard this as an unnecessary waste of time but it makes the process less hazardous, puts control on the possession and hardly uses up any time at all.

One aspect of lineout play that does not get enough practice time is the opposition mess-up ball mentioned earlier. Practise and refine your team's reactions to opposition errors at the lineout, an area of the game that is notorious for mistakes. If you were to fall on and claim 75% of lineout mistakes in every game, you would probably win the lineout stats each week. So build in errors at training and do not allow your front man to turn his rear end to the touchline. He should be watching the throw and the lineout at the same time. On the opposition ball he can turn fully to the lineout only when he ascertains that they are not throwing to their front man and on his own team's throw in he should be ready for a pass from his own thrower-in if his opposite number is not looking at what is going on at the throw. It is so obvious, yet week after week at all levels of the game you see the front man facing fully infield with his hands on his knees; his hands should be ready to do something and he should be watching the game in front of him before he goes completely to full-lineout mode.

A useful ploy that the coach can use to sharpen awareness and peripheral vision at the lineout is to carry a spare ball throughout all lineout practices, and the rule is that this ball becomes the priority over anything else when (and only when) it hits the ground. The coach will occasionally let it drop and the players have to spot that and claim the 'mess-up' ball as their possession. This has to be achieved while they are simultaneously concentrating on the lineout practice, which is not too far removed from what happens in a game. The coach can also dummy the odd ball so that the fringe players who are not lifting or jumping are forced to concentrate on the lineout as well as the potential glory of winning the loose ball.

Just one more Lineout. If seasoned coaches could have a pound for each time this has been begged for, they'd be rich men. Unfortunately, it never is just *one* more lineout and the whole thing can plod on and on – usually when the coach has the rest of the team (i.e. the backs) twiddling their thumbs waiting for the team run.

Knock this one on the head as soon as it first appears as the forwards will always find a reason (excuse?) for one more of just about everything that can be practised in isolation from the eyes of the backs, who themselves practise the 'just one more' scenario when the forwards are waiting for their regal presence.

If there is a split, let the various groups know how long they have and explain that a whistle will be blown five minutes before the end of that split. Be precise and call the team together as soon as the last five minute period is up. Make your future coaching organisation easier by coming down hard on this one right from the first session. If they want 'just one more', they can get together at the end of training, but it is curious that 'just one more' isn't quite as urgent at 8.30 p.m. as it had been an hour previously.

CHAPTER 9

RESTARTS

Don't ever finish the session with restarts, because that practice evening will never end if you say that you will all stay there till you get it right. The restart is the kiss of death on any session and the sooner you accept this, the better your practices will be. By all means say exactly how many you will be doing, but do not go beyond that number if things go wrong.

Why do teams persist in running the chasers (nearly always forwards) into the ground before it has been ascertained whether or not (usually not) the kicker can drop kick accurately most of the time? If the outcome of the kick is uncertain, go long and get a good chase on it. It is not pretty but it offers a greater percentage chance of success than the short one that is badly directed. If your opponents can score by running the ball back from their own 22, you are probably going to lose the game anyway – and they'd have scored even more quickly from a poorly directed short kick.

The chase of the long kick should probably have five in the first line of chase, comprising a combination of three or four backs and one or two faster forwards, which leaves plenty of backs to organise if the opponents kick back against you. A waiting deep line of three to retrieve kicks, (scrum half, full back and one winger?) would make the opposition think twice before aimlessly kicking back. The rest of the forwards should be spaced between the first chasing line and the kick-retrieval line of three at the back.

Rather than aimless sprinting to retrieve long restarts in training, try to get structure and organisation into where everybody will go and try to get them all aware of what is likely to occur.

If the opposition do kick straight back to you, the dilemma then is what to do next in counter attack. The simplest advice to the player who receives the kick is to head immediately for where the ball came from and/or where the greatest number of opposition players seems to be grouped. It is not a bad blueprint for any counter-attack strategy and could serve your players well. It is all very well to invite your counter attacking players to look for space, but it easier for them to quickly scan for opposition numbers then head for that area; space will start to emerge from that direction of thrust.

If their restart from the middle does not go 10 metres, be very careful before insisting on playing it as once you touch it, the ball is in play and you may not gain much from their error. However, consider this. Why not take the scrum as you have to be pretty inept not to win that ball cleanly. Now your No 8 will see right side pick up, dummy, shimmy, show of genuine pace and No 8 scores with no assistance. Immediately disabuse him of this foolish optimism and become pragmatic. Get your longest/most accurate kicker to poke a long kick to a corner straight from the scrum and chase it hard. With a good chase you might be pleasantly surprised how much yardage you make. You can usually end up with a lineout in their 22, pre-call/arrange what you will be doing, win an early ball and pose a threat to the enemy goal line. This has, from my experience, a greater chance of success than the no 8's solo performance that all too often gets more marks for artistic impression than for content or success.

It also gets at the opposition's mental resources as they will be none too happy if a badly-struck restart from the middle ends up with their defending a lineout in their own 22. There could be just a little discord between the eight forwards and their own restart expert. Taking the scrum reinforces their annoyance with their inept kicker.

When you have a long restart strategy, you must ensure that you also find a kicker who can put a short kick on the button. The long kick will be relatively safe with a proper chase, but you will need options once you identify your kicker and the short restart does become an option.

If you go short left, it is best if you have one or two chasers who can actually go up for the ball with their left hand; similarly you need right hand-up jumpers on the right. If they go up with the wrong hand, they almost have to turn their back on the ball to try to make contact. Yet time after time you see teams restarting left simply because the kicker likes that side best, when nobody in the chase is naturally left-handed or proficient in the left-hand take.

If the ball cannot be caught, then you need a designated player to go behind their receiving jumper so that you can claim any badly tapped ball from them. Remember that, as long as the chaser was onside at the kick, there is no offside at any stage of the restart process until a tackle has been made, and/or a genuine ruck or maul has been formed – so cash in on their mistakes if they make them!

You will need a jumper to go for your own kick and a support player directly behind him for the tap. When you are receiving, avoid lifting your jumper until it has been perfected to the Nth degree. The professionals make it look easy but it is potentially dangerous for part-timers. Just watch some of your forwards try to guess where the restart is going then fear the worst if you have to get three of them in the right spot at the right time with a perfect lift that is synchronised completely with the trajectory of the ball. Play safe and let one player jump for the ball then get the support up and into him as soon as he touches it.

Once you are satisfied that your kicker can put the restart exactly where you want it, there are some simple strategies that may be used to confuse the opposition. The first is to consider using a strong back to go up first for the ball. He will probably get there quicker than any forward and, if he can collect the kick cleanly, could be a threat to the defence right from collection. A 4/4 left and right split can ring the opposition alarm bells, especially when it is pre-called and the players go very quickly to their side. The kicker can quickly assess the opponents' readiness and restart according to what he sees; if there is an obvious state of unreadiness, go to that side of most confusion.

Once the split 4/4 is ready to go, there could be a dink just forwards and just to the side of the kicker.They are unlikely to have more than one player guarding this area and there are two options: (i) They catch, your centre (or designated player) tackles him, gets up immediately, straddles the defender and takes the ball. There is a very good chance of the defender being penalised at this stage or you could win the ball at the tackle and play from there. (ii) Your player catches the restart and you attack. Again, as with most things, it needs practice, but it could get possession in an area where the opposition is not numerically strong.

I advocate a long ball strategy until you can get the restart kickers to practise so that a short kick can be a safe and sensible option.

CHAPTER 10

STATISTICS

Fitness testing

You may be tempted into thinking of fitness testing to find out more about your players. This is a potential minefield as you have to ask yourself a number of questions, not least – why do you need the information, how are you going to get it and what are you going to do with it once you have it?

The elite game has vast amounts of time to test throughout the season, but you are likely to be limited. They also have experts who can work on perceived weaknesses, but you are unlikely to have too much help. And even if you had assistants, would the players see this as a valuable use of time?

You have to be pragmatic. If, for instance, you have a tight-head prop who is obviously very unfit but is the best man in the club at locking-out a scrum, are you really going to drop him because of poor fitness levels?

You can test for just about any aspect of fitness, but for tests to be reliable there has to be equipment, accurate description and scrutiny of the exercises and a willing work-force of players and assistant coaches. If you want to test speed, you will probably get odd results if you do not have state of the art timing kit with light beams rather than starting and finishing lines. Try defining an acceptable press-up, sit-up or pull-up and you will wonder if it is really necessary.

That does not mean that there is no place for fitness testing in any club's programme, but you must decide what you are trying to test, how it can be done accurately then what you will do with the information once it has been compiled.

Match statistics through video

You may have an expensive system that allows you to get a copy of individual players' performances and this is a fantastic tool for professional teams. Players can be shown what they did and they can study their own performance for as long as they wish, but they will expect some feedback from the coaching staff then remedial work/coaching if that is necessary.

However, community rugby teams are more likely to have only a video of the game and it is up to the coach to do with it what he can. Whatever he decides to do, it is time-consuming as the tape will have to be studied for a long period if anything good is to come from it. Then there is the problem of getting relevant clips to show the players, as they will not watch the whole video with total attention; they will be looking for their own cameos rather than coaching issues.

Video also requires time not only from the coach who analyses it, but also from the players who have to watch it in a fairly formal meeting. Once they simply play it when a few get together, the real potential coaching gains are virtually lost. If it is to be seen by the team, or parts of the team, the coach needs to be directing what is viewed and what the group is looking for. The 'we are watching the video of the game' is too loose, too vague; make the viewing specific in what you want them to look for.

There is a very simple method of utilising video of the game that is rough and ready, but it is not too time-consuming for the coach and it does give some pretty quick feedback to the players. When you watch the video, have a dictaphone and talk through all the good and bad points that you see from individuals and units and add a simple tick or cross in comment. You may end up with a list that sounds like:

15 x weak attempt tackle 2nd minute.

Scrum √ pushed them off ball 4th minute.

12 √ big tackle 5th minute.

Backs x slow up in line of defence at their 1st try 10th minute.

10 √excellent kick to relieve pressure 14th minute.

You will end up with a very long list of points that you have noted, then you simply replay the dictaphone and write out each person's comment on his personal sheet. You end up with a set of comments on each player and some playing units (though some may not be mentioned each week) with a very rudimentary tick and cross system against each of the comments.

The full back, for instance, may end up with a set of comments that looks like:

X weak attempt tackle 2nd minute.

X dropped high ball 4th minute.

√ Hit line well 10th minute.

√ Tackle 12th minute.

√ Relieving touch finder 16th minute.

X Did not protect blindside 22nd minute at their try.

√ Excellent penalty 26th minute from long range.

And so on.

This is a simple system, though it does take time for the coach. He will improve his own scanning skills as he does it more frequently and it does not require vast sums of money. However, it does show trends even if it is not sophisticated. If you keep copies of each player's sheets, you will notice that some faults keep on coming – as do displays of skills. This information, though simple, might be useful in how you coach individuals and units and how you form strategies each week. A full back who fumbles the high ball on one wet and windy Saturday may have had an off day; a full back who fumbles the high ball most weeks might need to be dropped or relocated.

This use of video also allows you to have a tackle chart in the changing room. This will promote debate, occasionally outrage. But go for it! The top-of-the-table tacklers will love the system as their hard work is being recognised; the less than brave will moan, whinge and cavil on what the definition of a tackle is. However, whatever the definition of a tackle is, they aren't making many.

This chart may just promote an in-team competition to do better at tackle contact. You will not get a born-again coward to knock all and sundry over, but he might be encouraged to scrag somebody, which could be a major breakthrough in his definition of contact. If such a player does down an opponent, however far from a textbook tackle it might be, make a big deal of it and ensure that the feat is recorded on the chart with no loss of time. This player might have performed an act of bravery that he previously thought impossible.

In fitness testing and in match statistics, do not allow yourself to become bogged down with 'facts'. The most effective coaches do not necessarily have reams of data and they will use the information sensibly. Do not let the tail (statistics) wag the dog (coaching and playing). It has been said many times that it is very easy to induce paralysis by analysis; don't fall into the trap but be open-minded and innovative about what you really do need, what is possible and how you plan to use it for the benefit of your team.

SUMMARY

This book, I hope, will offer practical advice to you in your coaching. Rugby is essentially a game where players stay on their feet with the ball off the ground. The possession, once secured, has to go forward or your team will be running backwards for long periods of the game.

Your coaching philosophy will have to to be conditioned to hold a practical element, especially if you do not have the skills available to play in a certain way that you might ideally like. You can only play with the talent available in your individuals and in the team, yet many coaches fail to recognise this and attempt strategies that are beyond the players' capabilities.

Right from your very first session with the players, look out for the one who can score; if you are lucky, you may find more than one! This type of player is worth his weight in gold and it is your responsibility to get him into the game as often as possible and you should not be guilty of allowing him to languish away from the action. Plan to get him into potential scoring mode as often as possible.

The technical skills of the game are relatively simple to master, but the tactical skills of how to use that possession are much harder to coach and refine. Try to offer advice to players all through your coaching sessions on what to do once the ball has been won – and discuss match situations as often as you can with your key decision-makers after all matches.

You may find that 'coaching' drills is a safer area than trying to coach tactical skills, but you will be rewarded many times over if you do try to improve players' habits once the ball is with your team and how you use it.

And when you are coaching, try to be aware that different players learn differently. Some players can pick up a move from a flip-chart presentation; others will be comfortable with a spoken set of instructions; and there are those who will need to jog through it to learn. Make sure that you are always aware that there is another group - those who will need a combination of all three learning methods before being able to give you a flat-out execution of that skill, move or play. Players, like people generally, have different methods of learning and your coaching will become more effective when you take this on board.

You will find that you become more than a coach as you will have to be a selector, man-management expert and motivator as well. However, this all channels into an effort from you to let your players reach their potential under your guidance

Do enjoy your coaching and, whenever possible, try to coach the essentials of the game in as simple a manner as possible. Avoid looking for complicated 'add-on' factors; the basics, done well, are usually quite good enough. If you are coaching away from the full-time professional level, your time available with the players will not allow too much more than a regime where simple things are coached to their maximum potential for individuals and for the team.

Good luck!

ACKNOWLEDGEMENTS

Stephen Jones, Editor, for encouragement and advice on the publishing world.

His book Endless Winter (Mainstream) won the 1994 William Hill/ Sportspages Sports Book of the Year. He has also written Midnight Rugby (Heinemann) and On My Knees (Mainstream) and edited the Rothams Rugby Yearbook for a decade.

He has coached at Maidenhead RFC for 12 years and is currently with the U17s.

RFU for the use of the diagrams compiled when I edited Technical Journal.

Steve Johnson for his advice on fitness skills.

Bob Kidman for his enormous assistance and advice on the way to getting the book published.

Photographs – Hartpury College.

Don Rutherford, O.B.E., (RFU Director of Rugby 1969-1999) for his encouragement to coaches and coaching.

Peter Thorburn, New Zealand, for encouragement and rugby advice.

Proof reading - Clive Leeke.

Website design – Paul Telford at www.smartermadeeasy.co.uk

Diagrams - Scott Woodhouse sw-design@virginmedia.com

Book layout and design – Regina Morrison at hotcotbern@hotmail.com

The many players and coaches I have been lucky enough to work with.

NOTES

NOTES